COUNTRY
CROCHET &
KNITTED LACE

COUNTRY CROCHET & KNITTED LACE

A CREATIVE GUIDE
WITH PROJECTS FOR CROCHET
AND KNITTED LACE

JAN EATON

NEW
HOLLAND

First published in the UK in 1994 by
New Holland (Publishers) Ltd
37 Connaught Street, London W2 2AZ

ISBN 1 85368 227 6

Editor Coral Walker
Assistant editor Sue Thraves
Art director Jane Forster
Photographer Steve Tanner
Illustrators Stephen Dew and Coral Mula

The author would like to thank the following:
Janet Bentley and Shelagh Hollingworth for their invaluable
work writing and charting patterns from historical pieces of
knitted lace and crochet
Annette Claxton and Jane Easson-Brown for their help and
encouragement
Clare Hayes for lending the Shetland shawl on page 2
DMC Creative World for supplying sample threads
Framecraft for supplying the crystal jar on page 116

Typeset by Ace Filmsetting Ltd, Frome, Somerset
Reproduction by Scantrans Pte Ltd, Singapore
Printed and bound in Malaysia

FOREWORD

The techniques of crochet and knitting have a fascinating history stretching back throughout the centuries. Today both crafts are undergoing a revival in popularity, particularly making lace. The basic techniques are easy to learn, consisting of several simple stitches and yarn movements, but as with all other textile crafts, practice makes perfect!

Both crochet and knitted lace are inexpensive to make yourself, requiring little in the way of equipment apart from a hook or pair of needles and ball of yarn. Both are easily transportable. Many people crochet or knit on a bus, train or plane journey, or to keep their hands occupied while chatting, listening to the radio or watching television. Try to prevent your current piece of lace from getting dirty when you have stopped working by wrapping it in an old, clean pillowcase or offcut of white cotton fabric and always make sure that your hands are clean before starting to work.

This book contains a variety of project designs for all levels of expertise for working in crochet and knitting. Also included is a pattern library giving instructions for more stitches and designs for each technique. Many of these extra designs can be substituted for those used in the project patterns. Each project is accompanied by a degree-of-difficulty symbol showing you which projects are suitable for beginners and which require an advanced level of skill. Be guided by these symbols when choosing a project to make.

Practical help, taking you through each technique – from working the basic stitches and selecting yarn and equipment, to pinning out and starching your finished piece of lace – is given in the introductory and finishing techniques chapters.

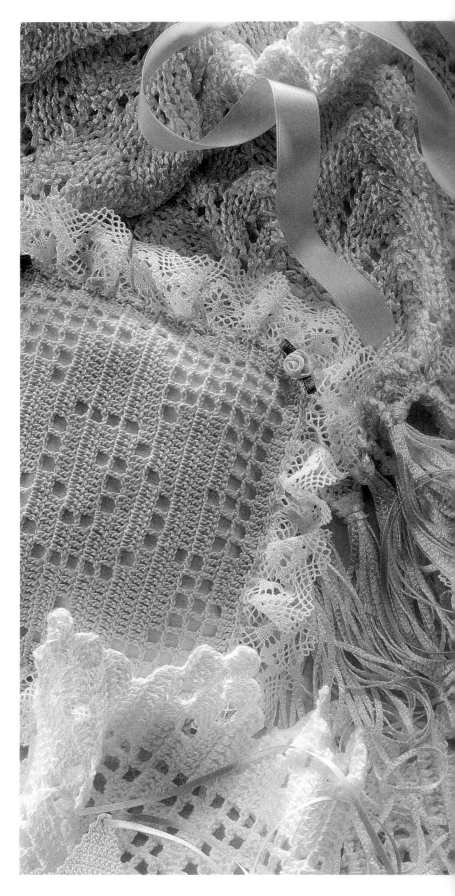

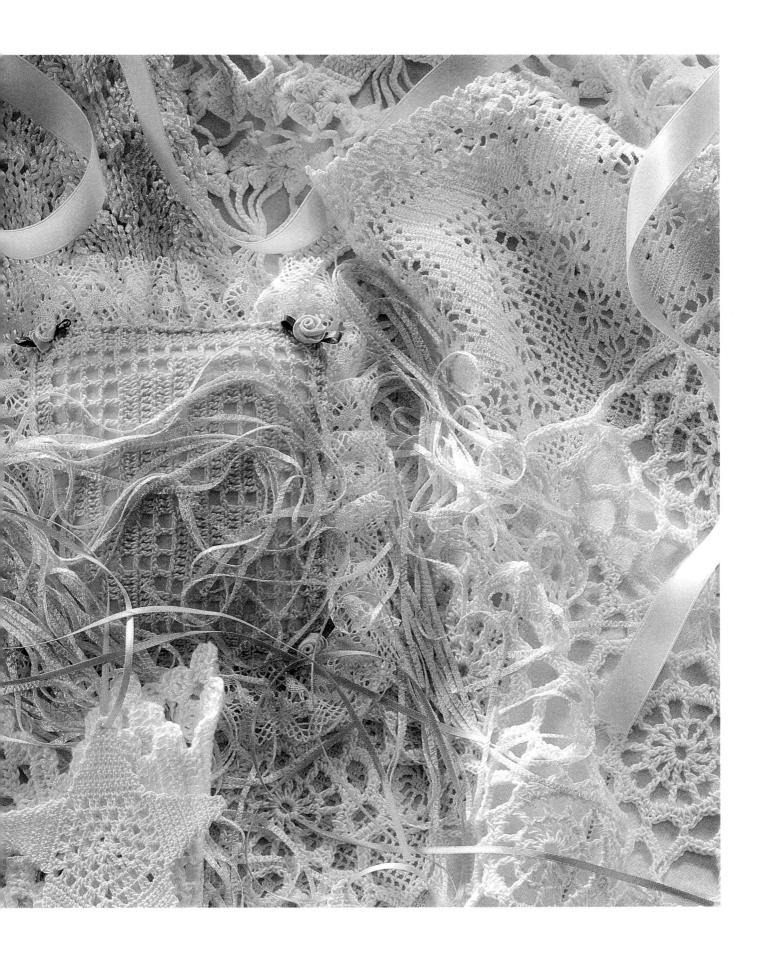

The craft of crochet

The craft of crochet has been practised for centuries to make garments and furnishings for both the home and the church. Crochet is known throughout the world: it is worked in countries from Europe to South America and China to the Middle East, using a variety of materials, styles and patterns to produce textures ranging from gossamer-fine, ornate lace to sturdy, woollen fabrics.

The basic stitches of crochet lace are simple to work and you will quickly become familiar with the various techniques which are involved. Whether making a length of intricate edging in fine cotton yarn to edge a snowy white table-cloth or working a pretty bag in thick yarn, the stitches and techniques you will use are exactly the same. Always use the best quality yarn you can buy and look after the finished item to make sure that you can use and enjoy your crochet lace throughout the years.

A LOOK BACK IN TIME

Crochet, like knitting, is a looped fabric made from a continuous length of yarn. Unlike knitting – where a multiple of stitches are worked on two needles at any one time – crochet uses a short hook on which one stitch is worked at a time. The term 'crochet' is thought to come from the French word *croc*, meaning a hook, but its origins are impossible to trace with any accuracy as very few early pieces exist today. Unlike pottery, metalwork and even glass, the various forms of textile crafts, particularly those made for everyday domestic use and wear, have not survived in great numbers over the centuries due to the impermanent nature of the fibres used.

Some schools of thought believe that the origins of crochet and knitting were the same, possibly invented in the Middle East, and that the techniques are linked by a type of crochet called Tunisian crochet which is worked on a long hook in a similar way to knitting. Others suggest that the two crafts developed independently. Whatever the exact origins, the early fragments of crochet which are known to exist have been found in places right across the world from Europe to Africa, China to Turkey and the United States to South America.

Crochet can be worked to have two very different appearances. Using fine yarn and fine hooks, the resulting fabric is light, open and can compete on its own terms with the finest bobbin and needle-made laces. Crochet can also be worked in thick woollen yarn on large hooks to produce a heavy, densely-worked fabric. This heavier crochet appears to have been the most widespread of the two types.

The Chinese made three-dimensional, sculptured crochet dolls, African tribes worked ceremonial headgear for their chiefs and in Scotland, warm caps and cloaks were fashioned for shepherds to wear when tending their sheep in the fields. In some parts of Scotland, crochet is also known as 'shepherd's knitting'.

Crochet lace probably originated in Italy during the sixteenth century. Worked extensively during this period by nuns to make wonderfully ornate church vestments and trimmings, crochet was also known as 'nun's lace'. Italian crochet lace was worked in very fine cotton yarn using tiny ivory or bone hooks, and knowledge of the technique spread gradually through the Roman Catholic world across Europe to Spain and Ireland.

By the nineteenth century, crochet lace was used to trim garments and linens in the wealthiest households. The techniques were liberated from the confines of the European church largely due to the enthusiasm of a French émigré, Eleanore Riego de la Branchardière, who settled in Ireland

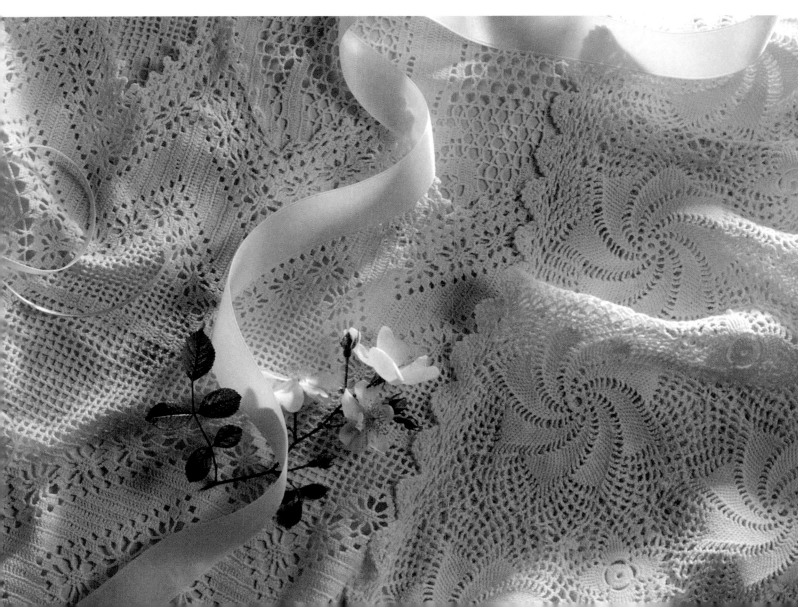

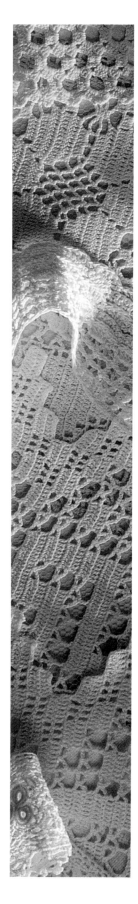

and was fascinated by the fine crochet laces made by the nuns in Dublin convents. She learnt how to work this very intricate crochet lace and invented many new and interesting stitches and patterns which she published in the secular magazine she founded called *The Needle*.

In the mid 1840s when the potato crop, the staple food of the Irish, failed and potatoes rotted in fields all over Ireland, many women and children were able to earn money by making crochet lace as well as doing other kinds of 'fancy needlework' including knitting and embroidery. They were taught the necessary skills and organized by nuns, who supplied the materials and marketed many of the finished products. Irish crochet lace of this period was of a very high quality and imitated the appearance of expensive, handmade European laces.

A distinctive type of fine crochet with relief motifs of roses and shamrocks worked on a delicate lattice background began to be worked in Ireland during this period, primarily as the result of two home industry schemes set up for peasant women by Mrs Porter in Carrickmacross and Mrs Hand in Clones. Often called Irish crochet, this type of crochet lace is also known by its places of origin, as Carrickmacross lace and Clones lace.

Irish crochet patterned with leaf, rose and shamrock motifs is still worked today and is used to make decorative insertions and edgings for garments and linens as well as complete items such as bedspreads and tablecloths.

Examples of antique Irish lace command high prices when they come up for auction – this is usually a rare occurrence as most fine pieces are greatly prized and handed down from generation to generation. Many of the Irish peasant women who worked fine crochet lace emigrated to the United States with their families to make a new life away from the poverty of their famine-stricken homeland and they passed on the techniques, stitches and designs they had learned.

During the second half of the nineteenth century, crochet lace was in vogue in Britain and the colonies – Queen Victoria accepted gifts of Irish crochet lace to trim her gowns and the popularity of the new type of lace spread rapidly across Europe from court to court. Queen Victoria actually learned to crochet and was often seen working crochet lace patterns in public. Books of crochet patterns were published in Europe and the United States and designs appeared in all the women's magazines of the day from the British *Woman's Magazine* to the American *Godey's Lady's Book*.

Weldon's Practical Crochet was a series of practical magazines published in England around 1895 and available by yearly subscription 'post free to any Part of the World'. The variety of patterns is breathtaking – from 'How to Crochet 47 Useful Articles for Ladies, Gentlemen and Children', including slippers, quilt squares, shawls, a boy's cricketing cap and a cosy antimacassar, to 'New and Original Designs for Mantel Valances, Brackets, Borders for Sideboard Cloths, Piano Covers etc' worked in coloured yarn over pre-formed moulds.

FILET CROCHET

During this peak of popularity, the most sought after designs were for a crochet lace technique called 'filet crochet' using areas of light and shade to create a realistic or abstract design. Today, filet crochet is still worked extensively throughout Europe and the United States.

A versatile form of crochet, filet crochet is based on a regular, square grid or network. It is extremely simple to work, as the technique uses only the basic chain, double crochet and treble stitches. The grid serves as the background for geometric and figurative designs which are created by 'filling in' some of the spaces of the grid with blocks of treble stitches to create areas of light and shade. Lacets and bars are variations on the grid which create a more open, lacy surface.

The true filet lace is an expensive, hand-knotted net, made with a netting shuttle, which has designs darned on it using a needle and thread. Filet crochet, originally worked as an inexpensive substitute for this time consuming, hand-made lace, gives a similar, slightly coarser result, but the work requires less skill and dexterity than true filet lacemaking.

Filet crochet designs are expressed in chart form and originally ranged from simple repeated geometric motifs to large landscapes and pictorial scenes, complete with human figures, birds, flowers, fruit and animals.

Traditionally, this type of crochet was worked with fine hooks in fine white or ivory cotton and linen yarns to produce complex, large scale pictures often depicting a scene from the Classics or the Scriptures. As simple, bold lettering is also effective in filet crochet, many designs incorporated a text such as The Lord's Prayer or a religious maxim or educational verse similar to those found in embroidered samplers of the period.

CROCHET TODAY

Crochet lace is currently enjoying a revival and people are rediscovering the pleasures of creating a fine piece of lace by hand. The techniques are simple to master, and the craft requires little in the way of equipment apart from hooks and yarn. Once you have found a brand of hooks you are comfortable with, buy a complete set, preferably with a case so the required size is always to hand.

Some of the crochet lace pieces in this book, including the butterfly tablecloth (page 43) and hearts and diamonds bed-spread (page 46) have been in my family for many years. My maternal grandmother, who taught me how to crochet as a small child, worked large pieces of fine filet crochet to make curtains and edge table-cloths well into her seventies. Specific yarns, hook sizes and tension have not been quoted, but the patterns have been written and charted for you to recreate these heirlooms of your own. The yarn thickness hook size chart opposite will help you select your materials.

The remaining projects have been de-signed specially for this book, particularly with beginners in mind. The two country rose pincushions on page 55 make the ideal introduction to filet crochet, while the hexagon shape lavender bags (page 63) give the novice useful practice at working crochet in rounds. Each project is graded with a degree-of-difficulty symbol so you can tell at a glance which projects are suitable for your level of ability and skill.

The pattern library on pages 68-79 con-tains over 20 more stitch patterns for crochet lace including shell and openwork stitches for making shawls and wraps, a selection of motifs which can be worked and joined together in a variety of ways, and a selection of charts for filet crochet from small pictorial designs to alphabets for personalizing your household linen. Each section in the pattern library is introduced with suggestions for using specific stitches.

NOTE FOR LEFT-HANDED READERS
When following the diagrams for working crochet stitches and techniques, prop the book up in front of a large mirror so the diagrams are reflected in reverse (ie left-handed) form.

NOTES FOR NORTH AMERICAN READERS
Both metric and imperial measurements are used throughout the book and there is a hook conversion chart below. However, there are a few differences in crochet terminology and yarn names between the UK and the US. These are:

UK terms	US terms
Double crochet (dc)	Single crochet (sc)
Half treble (htr)	Half double crochet (hdc)
Treble (tr)	Double crochet (dc)
Double treble (dtr)	Treble crochet (tr)
Tension	Gauge

UK yarn names	US yarn names
3 ply	Lightweight
4 ply	Fingering or mediumweight
Double knitting	Sport
Aran weight	Worsted or fisherman
Double-double or chunky	Heavyweight or bulky

Chart for crochet yarn weight/hook size combinations

No 60 cotton	0.6 mm
No 40 cotton	0.75 mm–1 mm
No 30 cotton	1 mm–1.25 mm
No 20 cotton	1.25 mm–1.5 mm
No 10 cotton	1.5 mm–1.75 mm
4 ply	2 mm–3.5 mm
Double knitting	3.5 mm–4.5 mm
Aran	5 mm–6 mm
Chunky	6 mm–7 mm

Crochet Hook Conversion Chart

International Metric	British Old sizes (Aero)		American
	WOOL	COTTON	
0.6		7	14
0.75		6	12
1		5	10
1.25		4	8
1.5	16	3	7
1.75	15	2	4
2	14	1	0
2.5	12	0	B
3	10	3/0	C
3.5	9		E
4	8		F
4.5	7		G
5	6		H
5.5	5		–
6	4		I
7	2		K

Practical Skills

CHOOSING AND USING YARNS

There is a wide variety of yarns available which can be used to make crochet lace. Traditionally, this was worked in very fine cotton, linen or wool yarns but today almost any type of yarn with a smooth surface is acceptable. The weight of yarns you can use varies from the finest mercerized No 60 cotton to double knitting yarn. However, fluffy, hairy yarns such as mohair and textured, knobbly yarns are not successful; a lace stitch pattern worked in mohair will be indistinct, while one in textured yarn will pull out of shape owing to the knobs in the yarn.

Yarn is usually sold ready-wound into balls of a specific size and the amount contained in each ball is quoted by weight rather than by length. The weight is given in grams or ounces – the most common ball sizes are 25 g or 50 g (1 oz or 2 oz) – and the length of yarn in the ball will vary from yarn to yarn depending on thickness. Occasionally, yarn is sold in coiled hanks or skeins and this must be wound by hand into balls before you begin to crochet. Fine cotton yarn is sold in a small, flattened ball wound round a card or plastic and usually labelled with length as well as weight.

Pure wool and wool/synthetic mixtures are formed by twisting together a number of strands or 'plies'. The finished yarns are available in several weights, from fine 2 ply to heavy double-double knitting weight (also known as chunky). Use the quoted ply as a general guide to the thickness of the yarn, as yarn measurements are not standard from spinner to spinner and the thickness will vary according to the degree of twist as well as the fibre composition.

Thick cotton yarns are also available in two plies, 4 ply and double knitting. Many of the finer cotton yarns available in the shops are labelled as crochet cotton, and are particularly good for working crochet lace as these yarns are mercerized, making them smooth and very strong with a slightly glossy surface. The thickness of crochet yarns is quoted in a series of graded numbers, from the coarsest (No 3) to the finest (No 60).

For the beginner, double knitting wool or a wool/synthetic yarn is ideal for practising stitches, patterns and techniques. Wool retains a certain amount of stretch and 'give' when it is spun into a yarn and this makes stitches easier to work. Begin by using a 4 mm crochet hook with this weight of yarn. When you have become familiar with using the wool yarn, change to a smooth cotton yarn of about the same thickness and work your stitches in this, again using a 4 mm hook. Cotton yarn is harder on the fingers than wool and has

very little 'give' in it, but lace stitch patterns show up well. When you feel confident handling this weight of yarn and size of hook, move on to finer yarns and hooks. The chart on page 15 gives information about hook sizes and suggests yarn weight/hook size combinations.

Each ball of yarn is wrapped in a paper band (called a ball band) which gives you lots of useful information about the yarn. As well as fibre composition and the weight of the ball, it will also show the colour and dye lot number, symbols for washing and pressing and often a range of suitable hook sizes plus tension details. International yarn care symbols are shown on page 33.

The dye lot number on the ball band is particularly important as when the yarn is dyed in batches there are often subtle variations in colour between lots. Although this difference may not be apparent when you compare balls of yarn in your hand, it will probably show as a shade variation when the yarn is made up and may look unsightly. Always use yarn from the same dye lot for a single project.

Make sure you keep a ball band for each piece of crochet lace you work. Keep it in a small polythene 'grip-top' bag with any left-over yarn and label the bag with details of the item you have made, including hook size. You will then be able to refer to the washing instructions and have the correct yarn ready to make any necessary repairs.

CROCHET HOOKS AND OTHER EQUIPMENT

Standard crochet hooks are made from steel, aluminium or plastic in a wide range of sizes. Steel hooks are the finest and they are used for working with fine crochet cottons, while aluminium and plastic hooks can be used for all types of thicker yarns. Today, the old numerical system has been

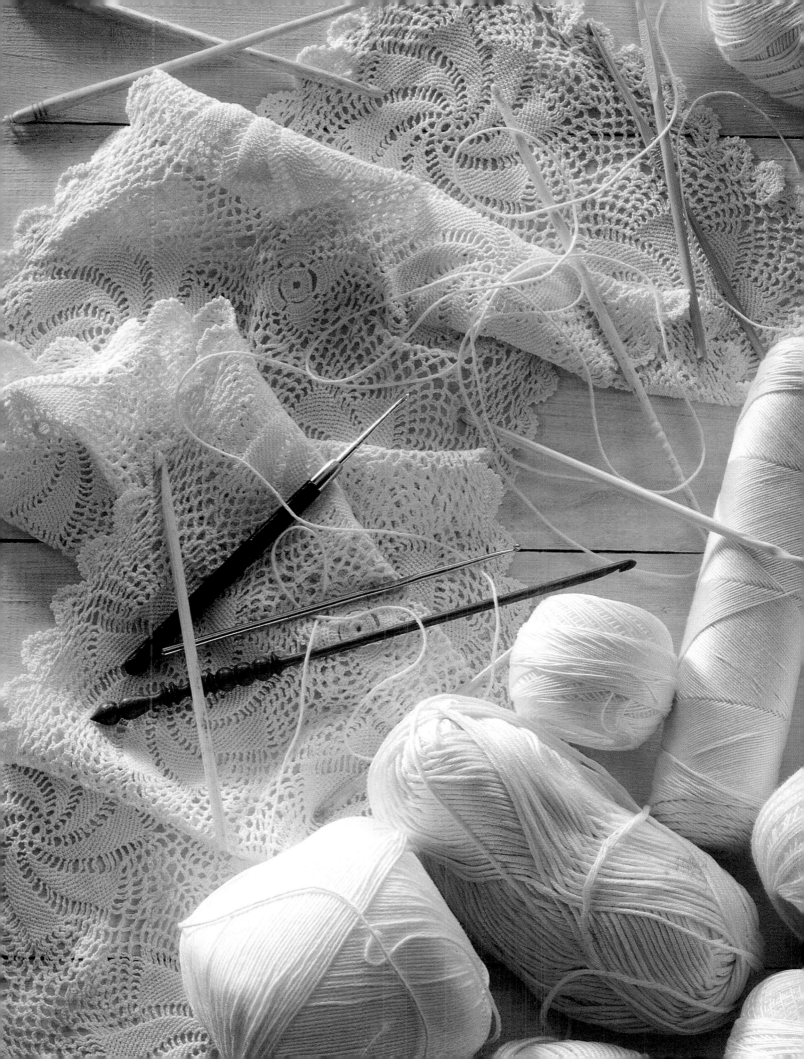

replaced by metric sizes and the hooks are marked with the size halfway down the shaft. The chart on page 15 gives the conversions from old to new hook sizes, as well as American sizes. Steel hook sizes range from 0.6 mm to 1.75 mm, aluminium from 2 mm to 7 mm and plastic from 8 mm to 15 mm.

As well as the standard hooks, steel hooks with chunky plastic handles are available. The sizes are identical to those of standard steel hooks, but the plastic handles make the hooks easier to grip and use if you have difficulty holding a fine hook. Continental wooden hooks are also available in a small range of sizes from 3.5 mm to 6.5 mm.

Row counter

A useful piece of equipment, the row counter is actually a knitting accessory which tells you the number of the row you are working; but one is just as useful when working crochet. The counter is a short cylinder with a numbered dial which is usually slipped on to one knitting needle close to the knob. When working crochet, keep the counter close by the pattern and turn the dial at the end of every row.

Markers

Split loops made from brightly coloured plastic can be clipped on to a crochet stitch to mark a place in the pattern. Short lengths of contrasting coloured yarn or bright embroidery cottons can be tied to a stitch to mark it instead.

Tapestry needles

Tapestry (also called yarn) needles have long eyes and blunt points. Keep a selection of sizes handy and use them when finishing thread ends and for sewing pieces of crochet lace together. Use ordinary sewing needles when applying a crochet edging, border or insertion to a piece of fabric.

Other equipment

Keep a bag or workbox handy containing general sewing equipment including sharp scissors, stainless steel pins with glass or plastic heads, a good quality dressmakers' tape measure, a selection of sewing needles and threads.

CALCULATING YARN REQUIREMENTS

As many of the crochet lace projects in this book were made in the early part of the century, the yarns used cannot be identified and are probably no longer available, so reliable guidelines to yarn quantities cannot be given. Keep in mind that the smaller projects, for example the country rose pincushions (page 55) and lavender bags (page 63), require less than 1 ball of yarn.

For the larger projects, such as the scalloped shelf edgings on page 52, the best way to calculate your yarn requirement is to crochet up one complete ball of your chosen yarn in the stitch pattern you wish to work, after first making small samples to check the compatibility of yarn and hook. At the end of the ball, pin out and block (page 30) your piece of crochet and let it dry completely. Next, check how many pattern repeats one ball of yarn has made and divide this figure into the total number of repeats you need. For example, if one ball of yarn makes 8 repeats of the pattern and you need to work 40 repeats in total, to make the desired length of edging you will need to buy 5 balls of yarn for each edging strip. Always buy slightly more yarn than you think you will need – odd balls can always be used up to make small items or whole balls of surplus yarn may sometimes be returned for a refund. Check with your supplier before purchase.

TENSION

When working a piece of crochet you must make sure that the fabric you produce is neither too loose and floppy nor too tightly worked and stiff. It is also important that the hook size you have selected is compatible with the weight of yarn you are using. This is called tension (also known as gauge) and is usually quoted as a number of rows and stitches over a given area of crochet fabric, usually 10 cm (4 in) square. When making a garment, correct tension is vital to ensure that the garment is the correct size when finished. Garment patterns include a tension guideline stating the number of rows and stitches which must be achieved. With items of home furnishing, the size is less crucial and the effect and handling quality of the finished crochet fabric is more important.

Because many different yarn weights can be used to make the projects in the book, specific yarns, hook sizes and tension cannot be quoted with any accuracy. The pattern instructions suggest a type of yarn, for example double knitting weight cotton, but you could substitute a finer yarn if you prefer. Apply commonsense when choosing yarn for a project – obviously the Christmas stars on page 66 would look less dainty and attractive worked in thick yarn, while the crochet bags on page 58 would be impractical worked in fine yarn on a large hook as they would not keep their shape when used. The chart on page 15 suggests various hook and yarn weight combinations and you can use this chart as a basis for your choice. Remember also that many yarns give a range of suitable hook sizes on the ball band.

Instead of working to a specific stitch and row count when working the crochet lace projects, make several small sample pieces with your chosen yarn and hook to check the results you will get before beginning to make the real thing. Crochet lace should be light and holey, but the crochet fabric should not be so loose that the stitches will pull out of shape when the article is handled. Remember that tension is a very individual thing – two people working with exactly the same pattern, yarn and hook will always produce slightly different results. As a general rule, if your samples are too tight and stiff, change to a larger size of crochet hook, while if the fabric is too loose and floppy, use a smaller size hook.

CROCHET STITCHES
Chain stitch (ch)

1 Begin with a slip knot on the hook, then wrap the yarn over the hook as shown. Unless otherwise stated, always wrap the yarn round the hook in this way.

2 Draw the yarn through to make a new loop without pulling the previous loop too tight.

Slip stitch (ss)

Insert the hook in the work, wrap the yarn over the hook, then draw the yarn through both the work and the loop on the hook in one movement.

Double crochet (dc)

1 Insert the hook into the second chain from the hook (one turning chain made), wrap the yarn over the hook and draw the yarn through the work only so that there are now two loops on the hook.

2 Wrap the yarn over the hook again and draw the yarn through both loops on the hook.

Half treble (htr)

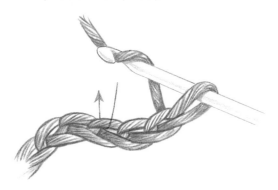

1 Wrap the yarn over the hook and insert the hook into the third chain from the hook (two turning chains made).

2 Wrap the yarn over the hook and draw the yarn through the work only so that there are now three loops on the hook, wrap the yarn over the hook again and draw through all three loops on the hook.

Treble (tr)

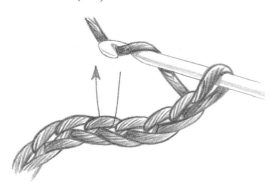

1 Wrap the yarn over the hook and insert the hook into the fourth chain from the hook (three turning chains made).

2 Wrap the yarn over the hook and draw the yarn through the work only so that there are now three loops on the hook.

3 Wrap the yarn over the hook and draw the yarn through the first two loops on the hook, wrap the yarn over the hook and draw the yarn through the remaining two loops on the hook.

To work two treble stitches together (tr2tog)
Work a treble, but omit the last part so that two loops remain on the hook. Work the second treble in the same way so that two loops remain on the hook. To complete, wrap the yarn over the hook and draw through all the loops on the hook.

Double treble (dtr)

1 Wrap the yarn over the hook twice and insert the hook into the fifth chain from the hook (four turning chains made).

2 Wrap the yarn over the hook and draw it through the work only so that there are now four loops on the hook.

3 Wrap the yarn over the hook again and draw it through the first two loops on the hook, leaving three loops on the hook.

4 Wrap the yarn over the hook and draw it through the next two loops only, wrap the yarn over the hook again and draw it through the remaining two loops on the hook.

Crossed double treble
The stitches forming a crossed double treble are worked in the same way as an ordinary double treble (above) but the two stitches are crossed, one behind the other.

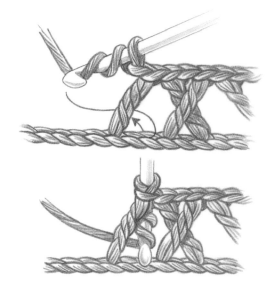

When the second stitch is worked, the hook is taken behind the first stitch before being inserted into the work.

MAKING A FOUNDATION CHAIN
Crochet stitch patterns are worked on a row of chain stitches, called the foundation chain or row. The number of chains to work for each pattern is given in the relevant instructions, but remember to work the stitches loosely and also to count the number of stitches correctly.

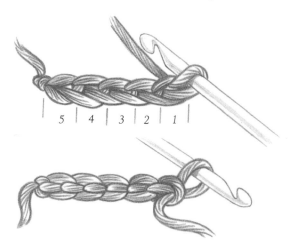

When counting the stitches as you make them, do not count the slip loop as a stitch, instead count each chain as you work it. When the foundation chain is finished, count the stitches again, this time counting the slip loop but ignoring the loop on the hook. Check that you are looking at the front of the chain when counting. The diagram shows both the front and back of the chain.

When the foundation chain is finished, turn and work the first pattern row into the chains as follows:

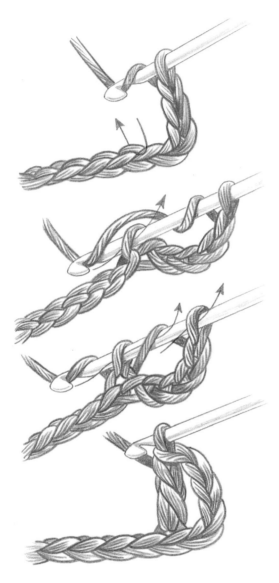

Turn the chain so the back of it faces you. Work the first row according to the pattern, inserting the hook into the centre of the chain as shown. This method makes a neat edge along the bottom of your work. The diagram shows a row of trebles being worked into the chain.

TURNING CHAINS

When working crochet in rows or rounds, you will need to work a specific number of extra chains at the beginning of each row or round in order to bring the hook up to the correct height for the stitch you are using. This is called a turning chain (starting chain when working in rounds) and the diagram shows the correct number of chains to work for each crochet stitch.

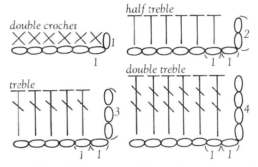

Usually, the turning chain (except in the case of double crochet where the single turning chain is ignored) is counted as the first stitch of the row. The number of chains to work is stated in each pattern in this book.

WORKING IN ROUNDS

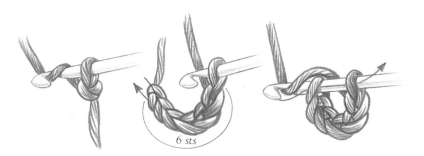

6 sts

To work crochet in rounds when making a square, round or shaped motif, begin by making a length of chain stitches and join the length into a ring. Count the stitches in the same way as for a straight foundation chain (above), and when you have worked the required number, join it into a ring with a slip stitch (see diagram).

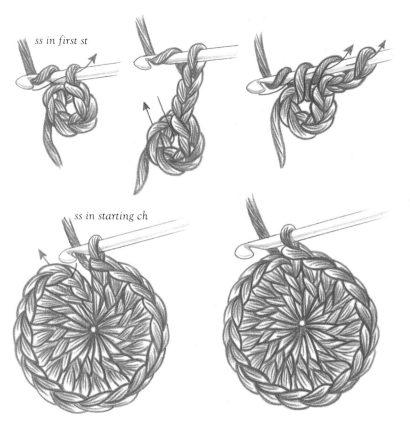

ss in first st

ss in starting ch

To begin the second round, work the correct number of starting chains (the diagram shows three starting chains as the round is worked in trebles). Continue the round following the pattern instruc-

tions, working each stitch into the centre of the ring, as shown. At the end of the round, join the first and last stitches with a slip stitch. Work subsequent rounds in the same way, beginning each one with the correct number of starting chain.

JOINING A NEW BALL OF YARN

Join a new ball of yarn at any point, making sure there is at least 10 cm (4 in) of the old ball left unworked. Knot the two ends together close to the work, then proceed in pattern as before, working the knot through to the wrong side when the join is reached. After you have finished the piece of crochet, go back and carefully undo any knots, then fasten off the ends securely with a tapestry needle as described on page 30.

FINISHING OFF

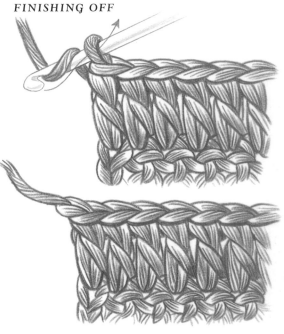

To finish off the yarn when a piece of crochet has been completed, make one chain then cut off the yarn, leaving a piece about 5 cm (2 in) long. Draw the end of the yarn through the chain and tighten gently. Fasten off the yarn end with a tapestry needle (page 30).

WORKING FILET CROCHET

Filet crochet is always worked from a chart and these are very easy to read as they show the pattern as it will appear from the right side of the work. Follow the numbered sequence at the sides of the chart, working from side to side and reading odd-numbered rows from right to left and even-numbered rows from left to right.

Each open square on a filet crochet chart represents one space on the grid. The space is formed by two trebles separated by two chains. When the chart square is filled with a dot, the two chains are replaced by two trebles to form a solid block of four stitches. Two blocks together on the chart are filled by seven treble stitches, three blocks by ten stitches and so on.

On some filet crochet charts, the blocks are indicated by crosses or solid squares rather than dots.

The foundation row is not shown on a filet crochet chart. Instead, to calculate the number of stitches needed in the foundation row, you will need to multiply the number of squares across the chart by three and add one. For example, for a charted design with 35 squares across, make a foundation row 106 chains long (35 × 3 + 1). You will also need to remember to add the appropriate number of turning chains, depending on whether the first chart row begins with a space or a block (see 'How to begin', below).

Lacets and bars are variations on the basic grid structure of blocks and spaces, and the variations create a pretty, more lacy effect.

A lacet or a bar is worked over two squares on the chart. On the chart, a lacet is shown as a 'V' shape and a bar as a horizontal line. Lacets are always worked in conjunction with bars, although bars may be used alone.

How to begin:

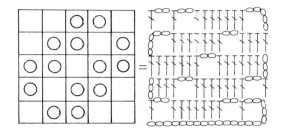

1 Begin by making the foundation chain as described above and start to follow the chart from the bottom right-hand corner. When the first square is a space, add four turning chains and work the first treble into the eighth chain from the hook. Continue working spaces and blocks along the row from right to left.

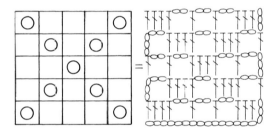

2 When the first square is a block, add two turning chains and work the first treble into the fourth chain from the hook, then work one treble into each of the next two chains and continue along the row.

To continue:

At the end of the row, turn the work and follow the second row on the chart, reading from left to right. Work spaces and blocks at the beginning and end of the second and subsequent rows as follows.

TO WORK A SPACE OVER A SPACE on the previous row, work 5ch (counts as 1tr and 2ch) – at the beginning of the row, miss first st and 2ch, 1tr into next tr, then continue working the spaces and blocks directly from the chart. At the end of the row, finish with 1tr into last tr, 2ch, miss 2ch, 1tr into 3rd of 5ch, turn.

TO WORK A SPACE OVER A BLOCK on the previous row, work 5ch (counts as 1tr and 2ch) – at the beginning of the row, miss first 3 sts, 1tr into next tr, then continue working spaces and blocks from the chart. Over the last 4 stitches at the end of the row, work 1tr into next tr, 2ch, miss 2tr, 1tr into top of 3ch, turn.

TO WORK A BLOCK OVER A SPACE on the previous row, work 3ch (counts as 1tr) – at the beginning of the row, miss 1st, 1tr into each of next 2ch, 1tr into next tr, then continue working spaces and blocks from the chart. At the end of the row, finish with 1tr into last tr, 1tr into each of next 3 ch of turning ch, turn.

TO WORK A BLOCK OVER A BLOCK on the previous row, work 3ch (counts as 1tr) – at the beginning of the row, miss 1st, 1tr into each of next 3tr, then continue working spaces and blocks from the chart. At the end of the row, finish with 1tr into each of last 3tr, 1tr into top of 3ch, turn.

Lacets form a 'V' shape in the basic grid. A bar is usually worked on the row above to restore the depth and rectangular shape of the grid, but can also be worked over a bar in the previous row to create a double space in the grid.

TO FORM A LACET: work 3ch, miss 2 sts on the previous row, 1dc into next stitch on previous row, 3ch, miss 2 sts, 1tr into next tr on previous row.

TO FORM A BAR: work 5ch, miss next lacet on previous row (or next two spaces), 1tr into next tr on previous row.

TO RETURN TO THE BASIC GRID above a bar on the previous row, work 2ch, 1tr into 3rd of 5ch, 2ch, 1tr into next tr.

Crochet abbreviations

ch chain
ss slip stitch
dc double crochet
htr half treble
tr treble
tr2tog work two treble stitches together
tr4tog work four treble stitches together
dtr double treble
st(s) stitch(es)
rep repeat
rem remaining
cont continue
alt alternate
beg beginning
foll following
patt pattern
sp space
* asterisk denotes that you must repeat a sequence of stitches from that point
[] the sequence of stitches enclosed inside square brackets must be worked as instructed
() round brackets contain extra information to help you, not instructions

Working lacets and bars

working lacets and bars in a pattern

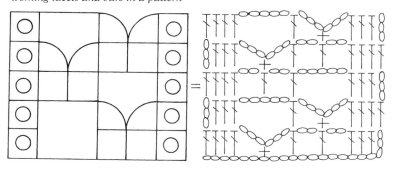

FOLLOWING A WRITTEN PATTERN

Crochet patterns are written in a logical way, even though at first sight the instructions can appear rather complicated. The most important thing to remember when following a pattern is to check that you start off with the correct number of chains in the foundation row or ring, and then work through *exactly* as stated.

Begin by reading the pattern before you start to crochet. As well as instructions, it will contain information about materials, measurements and finishing off the item. Although some instructions or details may not be clear on the first reading, the technique involved will be much easier to grasp once you begin work.

Crochet abbreviations are standard, see opposite; any special abbreviations are explained on the relevant pattern.

Asterisks

In order to make written patterns shorter and avoid tedious repetition, asterisks are used to indicate which sections of the instructions have to be repeated across a row. For example, an instruction such as '1tr into next st, * 3ch, miss 3 sts, 1tr into each of next 3 sts; rep from * to end' means that you begin the row by working one treble into the next stitch on the previous row, then work repeats of three chain, miss the next three stitches on the previous row, work one treble into each of the next three stitches right across the row until you reach the other side.

You will also find some instructions which tell you how to work any stitches remaining after the last complete repeat is worked. These will be similar to this instruction: 'rep from * to end, ending with 1dc into each of last 2ch, 3ch, turn'. In this case, after the last repeat has been worked, work one double crochet into each of the last two chain then work three chain and turn.

Square brackets

Square brackets fulfil a similar function to asterisks and both may be used in the same pattern row. Always repeat the sequence of stitches shown inside the square brackets as instructed before proceeding to the next instruction in the row. For example, a row reading '1tr into first st, * 2ch, miss 2 sts, [1tr, 3ch, 1tr] into next st; rep from * to end' instructs you to work one treble into the first stitch on the previous row, work repeats of two chain, miss two stitches on the previous row, work one treble, three chain and one treble into the next stitch on the previous row until you reach the end of the row.

Round brackets

Round brackets do not contain working instructions. Instead, they give extra information which you may find helpful; for example, by indicating the number of trebles made in a particular row by the time you reach the end.

Repeats

Each stitch pattern is written or charted using a specific number of pattern rows and the sequence is repeated until the work is the correct length. A simple pattern, such as the shelf edgings on page 52, is six rows long, while the deep edging on the crystal and silver tablecloth (page 36) requires 24 rows of crochet to work one complete pattern repeat. In some of the more complex projects – the butterfly tablecloth (page 43), for example – specific sections of the pattern are repeated. Where this is the case, the project instructions will tell you exactly which sections of the chart are to be repeated.

When working a complicated stitch pattern, always make a note of exactly which row you are working. Use a row counter or write the row number in a notebook with a pencil as it's very easy to forget where you are when your crochet session gets interrupted by the doorbell or a telephone call. Avoid the temptation to use a pen when making notes as ink is rather messy and can be very difficult to remove from light-coloured yarn.

FOLLOWING A CHARTED PATTERN

Many people prefer working from a chart rather than from written instructions. Although a charted pattern still contains some written instructions, the stitch pattern is expressed in visual form. Traditionally, British crochet patterns, with the exception of those for filet crochet, have been written rather than charted. However, there is now a strong movement towards the charted pattern which is used almost exclusively in other European countries. Charts also solve the problem of translating a long, complicated stitch pattern from one language to another.

To use a crochet chart, first familiarize yourself with the symbols and their meanings. These are explained in a key at the side of the chart. Each symbol represents a single instruction, such as double crochet or treble and indicates exactly where to work the stitch. Follow the numerical sequence shown on the chart whether you are working in rounds or rows.

In the same way as when using written instructions, keep a note of which row you are working at any one time using a row counter or notepad and pencil.

Crochet symbols

The chart shows the main symbols used in crochet charts. A key is also given beside each project and pattern library chart.

USING THE PATTERN LIBRARY

The pattern library pages give both written and charted instructions for a wide variety of crochet lace patterns. Filet crochet patterns are given as charts only.

o Chain *ch*

● Slip stitch *ss*

+ Double crochet *dc*

T Half treble *htr*

⊤ Treble *tr*

⊤ Double treble *dtr*

Many of these stitch patterns can be substituted for project designs, particularly the edging and border patterns. A selection of square motifs are given on page 70 which would make a lovely bedspread – work the motifs and join them together in the same way as the country cottage bedspread on page 40. The small filet crochet pictorial designs on page 79 can be substituted for the country roses charts on page 55.

To use the pattern library instructions for crochet lace worked in rows, begin by working the correct number of stitches in the foundation chain. For an edging, border or insertion, this number is given at the top of each pattern. Other patterns give you the correct number of chains needed to work one complete pattern repeat. For example, the first line of the large shell pattern on page 78 tells you to 'work a multiple of 10ch plus 2'. This means that the total number of chains to work so the pattern will be correct when finished must be divisible by 10, and you must also add two extra chains. So your foundation row could have say 62 chains (6 × 10 + 2) or 102 (10 × 10 + 2) and the pattern would be correct in either case. When working in rounds, the number of chain needed to make the ring is given with each pattern.

Making your own chart for filet crochet

You can easily adapt a simple squared chart (from Fairisle knitting or cross stitch, for example) for filet crochet by plotting the design on graph paper. Decide which areas are to be solid and fill these in with dots on the graph paper. The unmarked squares left indicate the grid background. One important point to remember, however, is that when working filet crochet from a square chart, the resulting piece of crochet is not likely to be perfectly square.

FINISHING TECHNIQUES

FINISHING OFF THREAD ENDS

Thread the end of the yarn through a tapestry needle and weave the point of the needle through several stitches on the wrong side of the work for at least 2.5 cm (1 in). Pull the needle and yarn through and cut off the yarn end.

PINNING OUT AND BLOCKING

This process is essential for bringing out the delicate patterns in crochet lace and it can be used safely with either cotton, wool or wool/synthetic mixture yarns as no heat is applied. Although blocking may seem rather a lengthy and tedious process, the time invested will be well spent.

To pin out and block crochet lace you will need a large piece of blockboard or chipboard covered with thick cork floor tiles, brown paper, drawing pins, a sheet of polythene, stainless steel pins with glass or plastic heads and a small plant sprayer filled with cold water.

Draw the outline of the piece on to the brown paper with a pencil – for a border draw two parallel lines, for a circular piece, draw radiating lines from the centre corresponding with the number of motifs in the pattern, and for a square or hexagonal motif draw the shape to the correct size. Pin the brown paper on to the board with drawing pins and cover it with the polythene sheet.

Spray the piece of crochet lightly with water and pin it out over the drawn shape using stainless steel pins. Don't be tempted to use ordinary dressmaking pins as these will rust and leave unsightly brown stains on the yarn. Adjust the pins until the crochet lace is stretched evenly, then spray with water once again, this time more heavily. Allow the crochet to dry completely at room temperature before removing the pins (this may take more than a day, depending on the yarn thickness). When you remove the pins, the crochet fabric will retain the shape in which it dried. When blocking a border or edging, you will need to work in several sections, letting the work dry before moving on to the next section.

JOINING MOTIFS

After pinning and blocking all the crochet motifs to the same size, join them together in one of the following ways:

Oversew (see diagram) square motifs together using the same yarn. Oversewing makes a very flat seam once it is opened out and pressed, unlike alternative methods which create an unsightly ridge.

Lay out the motifs to be joined in the correct order on a flat surface with the right side of each motif facing upwards. Working in horizontal lines, oversew the motifs together as shown, inserting the needle into a single loop of corresponding stitches. Secure the thread carefully at the beginning and end of the stitching.

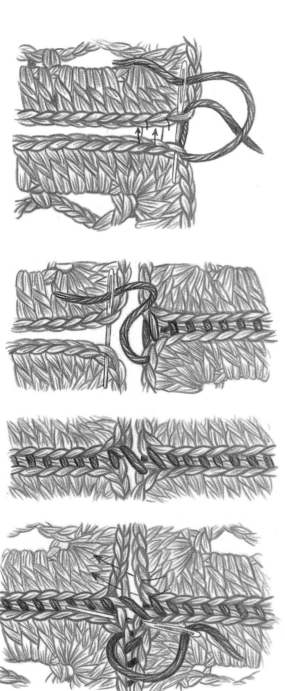

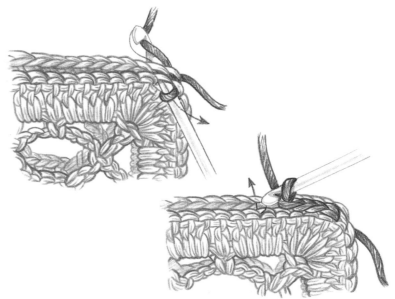

Place two motifs together with right sides facing and the edges to be joined aligning. Work a row of slip stitch as shown in the diagram, securing the thread at the beginning and end of the square. Repeat this with further motifs until you have a strip of joined motifs which is the required length. Make as many strips as you require, then join the strips together in the same way, taking care to match up the short seams across the strips.

Join lacy shaped motifs, like the snowflake shapes on page 49, by slip stitching them together at regular points round the edge of the motif. Complete the first motif, then work the second motif until you reach the last round. Following the pattern instructions, work the last round until you reach the point where the motifs are to be joined, place them together with right sides upwards and then join with a slip stitch as shown in the first diagram.

When all the horizontal seams have been stitched, repeat the oversewing to stitch the vertical seams. To make a stronger seam, you can insert the needle through both loops of corresponding stitches.

Alternatively, join square motifs together by **slip stitching** them together stitch by stitch.

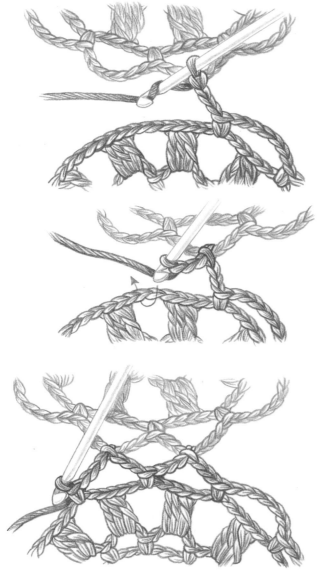

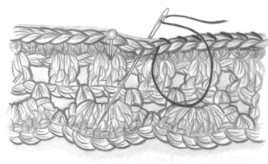

Using a tapestry needle and the same yarn that you used for the crochet, oversew (see diagram) the layers together. If you have used a very heavy yarn for the crochet, you will get a neater seam if you use a thinner thread, but don't be tempted to use sewing cotton as this will not be strong enough to take the weight of the crochet.

Crochet lace edgings and borders to fabric

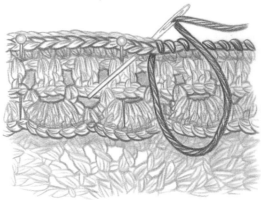

Continue in pattern, joining the two motifs together at the points indicated.

APPLYING BORDERS, EDGINGS AND INSERTIONS

A border to a crochet bedspread

Place the crochet border on top of the bedspread with right sides facing and straight edges aligning. Pin in place, distributing the length of the border evenly and gathering it slightly at each corner so that it will lie flat without pulling. Use long pins with glass or plastic heads so the pinheads will not pull through the crochet fabric.

Position the edging or border on top of the hemmed edge of the fabric with right sides facing and straight edges aligning. Make sure that the edging is evenly distributed and pin in place using glass-headed pins. Using a sewing needle and matching sewing cotton, stitch the crochet and fabric together using oversewing stitches (see diagram). Make small, neat stitches and take care not to pull the thread too tightly. When applying edging to a corner, gather the crochet slightly so that the edging will lie flat when stitched in position.

Adding insertions

Crochet lace insertions are applied between two pieces of fabric and are often used in conjunction with an edging or border.

Pin the top of the insertion to the first piece of fabric with right sides facing and proceed as above. Then pin the lower edge of the insertion to the second piece of fabric and sew in the same way.

Caring and storing

Follow the cleaning and pressing instructions on the ball band for the particular yarn you are using – a list of the international care symbols found on ball bands is given below. If the yarn you have used is machine-washable, put the item into a clean white pillowcase to prevent stretching during the machine cycle.

When not in use, store crochet lace wrapped in white, acid-free tissue paper in a cool and dry place. When folding a large item, pad the folds with tissue paper to prevent hard creases forming or, better still, roll it right-side out round a cardboard tube between layers of tissue paper.

With a little care, you can use and enjoy the crochet lace items you have made for years to come. Follow these guidelines:
○ Always wash crochet lace before it gets really soiled, taking prompt action to remove stains as soon as they occur, particularly on table-linen.
○ Repair holes and split seams as soon as possible to prevent further damage.
○ Keep items out of direct sunlight, especially during summer, as the sunlight will not only cause colours to fade, but will eventually weaken the fibres.

Starching crochet lace

Articles trimmed with crochet lace edgings benefit from being starched after laundering. Choose a stiff-finish starch for small items such as placemats and table runners and a soft-finish one for tablecloths and other items which will be draped or folded in use. The best method is to use soluble starch mixed with water. Dip the article into the starch solution, squeeze out the moisture, allow the item to dry then press with a hot iron.

Spray starch works well with small items, but take care when ironing as it can scorch when using a very hot iron.

Type of care	Dry cleaning	Washing	Bleaching	Drying	Ironing
Fairly easy care	(A) *Use any dry-cleaning fluid*	6/40° *Machine-wash at stated temperature*	Cl *Chlorine (household) bleach may be used*	○ *Can be tumble dried*	*High setting – hot*
Treat carefully	(P) *Use perchlorethylene or white spirit only*	30° *Hand wash at stated temperature*		*Dry on a line*	*Medium setting – warm*
Handle with great care	(F) *Use white spirit only*	*Wash by hand only*		||| *Allow to drip dry*	*Low setting – cool*
Do not use treatment shown	⊗ *Must not be dry-cleaned*	*Must not be washed*	*Do not use household bleach*	*Do not hang – lay flat*	*Must not be ironed*

Projects
in crochet

When selecting a project to make,
choose one which reflects your
present level of skill. Read right
through the instructions before you
begin to crochet. You will also find
it useful to work up one or more
sample pieces to check the effect of
your chosen yarn and hook.
The following projects are aimed at
people with varying levels of skill,
from outright beginners to more
experienced crochet enthusiasts.
You'll find a symbol with one, two
or three crochet hooks at the start of
each project. One hook indicates a
very simple design, two indicates
intermediate level and three hooks
are for more advanced projects
which should only be attempted by
a reader with considerable
experience and patience.

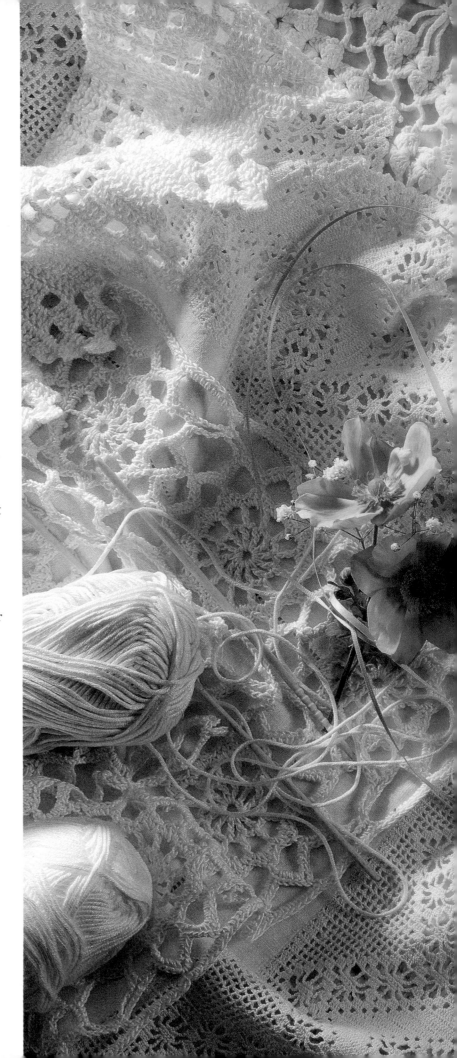

CRYSTAL AND SILVER TABLECLOTH

This attractive tablecloth is edged with a deep crochet border which has a pretty zigzag edge. The border is worked in fine cotton yarn and will take a considerable time to finish, but straight strips of the same design could be worked in a thicker yarn to decorate fluffy white towels for your bathroom. To do this, repeat the 24-row design from the chart until the strip is the correct length, making sure that both ends match. Stitch the strip to one short edge of the towel using matching sewing thread.

Materials
White fine crochet cotton, No 40
White cotton or linen fabric
Steel crochet hook 0.6 mm
White sewing thread
Sewing needle
Pins

Measurements
The original edging measures 15cm (6 in) deep. Work sufficient pattern repeats to make a border of the desired size to fit your table. When buying fabric, remember to allow a hem allowance of 1.5 cm (⅝ in) all round.

A deep border worked in fine cotton yarn edges this white linen tablecloth. Although the crochet is time-consuming to complete when using such fine yarn, the effect is exquisitely delicate and lacy.

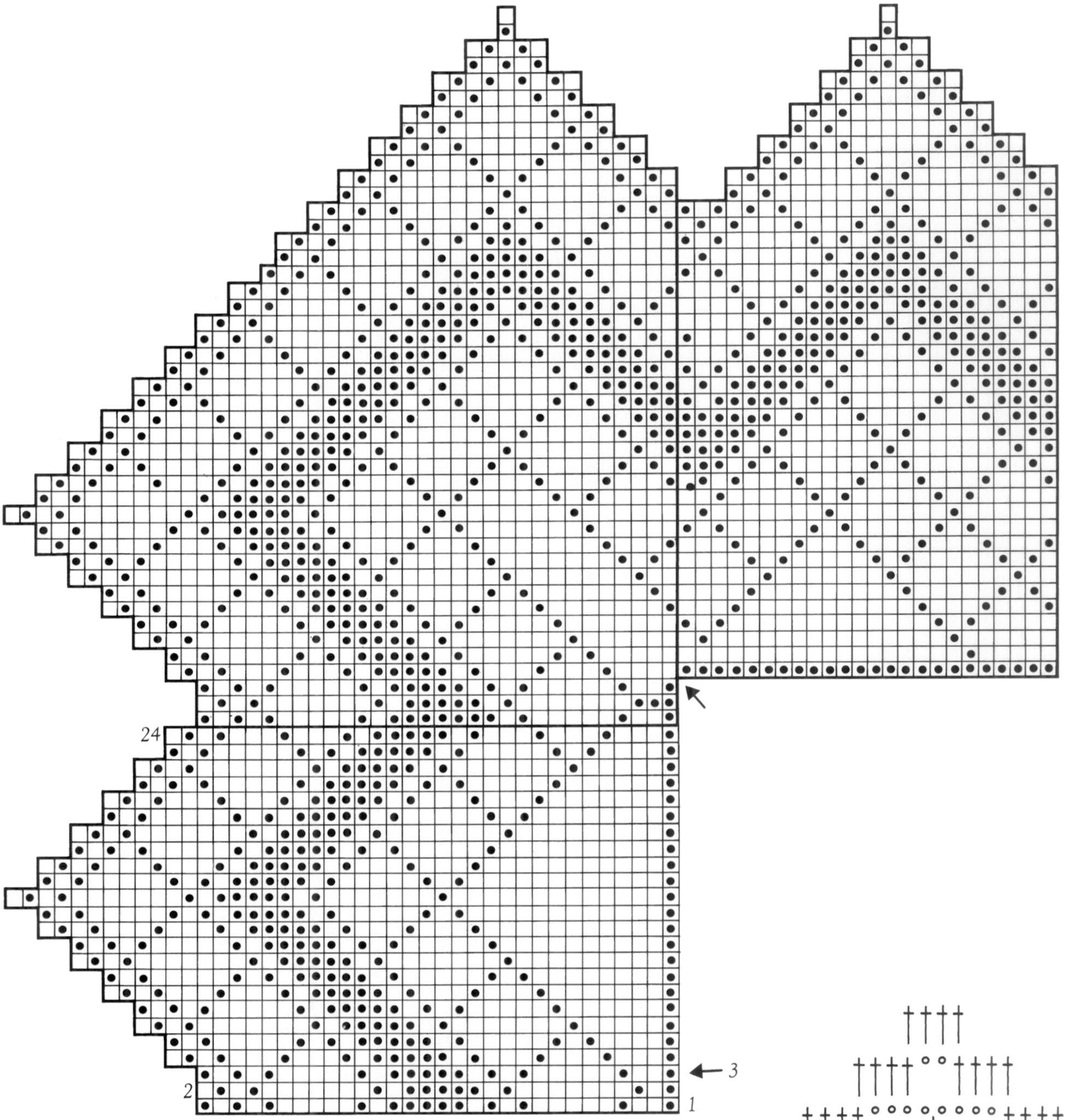

24

2

1

← 3

- ● | block – 4 tr
- ☐ | space – 1 tr, miss 2 sts, 1 tr
- ○ | ch
- + | dc
- † | tr
- ‡ | dtr

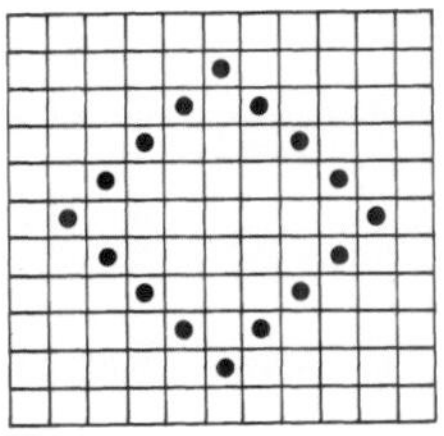

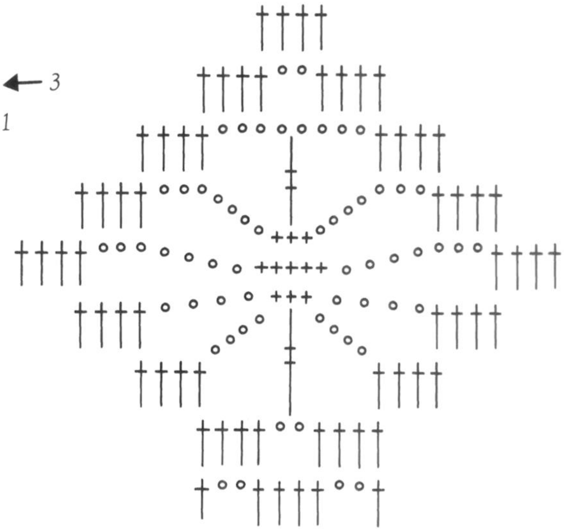

Abbreviations

A full list of crochet abbreviations is given on page 26.

To work filet crochet, see page 25.

Working the border

FOUNDATION CHAIN Work 87ch.

ROW 1 1tr into 4th ch from hook, 1tr into each of next 2ch, [2ch, miss 2ch, 1tr into next ch] twice, 1tr into each of next 3ch, * 4ch, miss 4ch, 1dc into each of next 3ch, miss 4ch, 1tr into each of next 4ch, 2ch, miss 2ch, 1tr into each of next 4ch *, 2ch, miss 2ch, 1tr into each of next 16ch, 2ch, miss 2ch, 1tr into each of next 4ch; rep from * to *, 2ch, miss 2ch, 1tr into each of last 4ch, turn.

ROW 2 5ch, miss 2tr, 1tr into next tr, 2tr into next tr, 2ch, miss 2tr, * 1tr into next tr, 2tr into sp, 1tr into next tr, 6ch, miss 3tr, 1dc into ch before 3dc, 1dc into each of next 3dc, 1dc into ch after 3dc, 6ch, miss 3tr, 1tr into next tr *, 2tr into sp, 1tr into next tr, 2ch, miss 2tr, 1tr into each of next 13tr, 2tr into sp, 1tr into next tr, 2ch, miss 2tr; rep from * to *, 2tr into sp, 1tr into next tr, 2ch, 1tr into each of next 3tr, 1tr into top of 3ch, turn.

Continue in pattern from chart until 24 rows have been completed. Repeat the 24 rows for the length of edging required until a corner is reached. Work to end within the heavy line.
Fasten off.

Rejoin at inner corner arrow. Continue in pattern working over row-ends. When work is completed, oversew top of last row to foundation chain.
Fasten off.

Making up the tablecloth

1 Sew in the ends. Pin out the border a section at a time following the illustrated instructions given on page 30. Spray with water and allow to dry completely before removing the pins.

2 Pin the border on to the fabric to check the fit and carefully cut away any surplus, remembering to leave a 1.5 cm (⅝ in) hem allowance round the edge. Remove the pins. Pin and tack a narrow double hem round the cloth and machine stitch or hem neatly by hand. Press the hem well on the wrong side.

3 Pin the border round the cloth, taking care to keep the points evenly spaced along each side. Using small, neat stitches, oversew the crochet border to the fabric. Press lightly on the wrong side with a warm iron.

COUNTRY COTTAGE BEDSPREAD

Thick white cotton yarn combined with a quick-to-work motif pattern creates a stunningly simple bedspread with a country feel. The perfect accessory for stripped pine furniture, the bedspread is worked in squares which contrast lacy and solid areas made from double crochet and double treble stitches. To show the motif pattern to full advantage, lay the bedspread over coloured bedlinen, choosing blue, deep crimson, green or old gold. Instructions and charts for alternative square motifs are given in the pattern library on page 70.

Materials
White double knitting weight
  cotton yarn
3.5 mm crochet hook
Tapestry needle size 22 or 24
Pins

Measurements
Each motif measures approximately 20 cm (8 in) square. You will need to make 63 complete motifs for the single size bedspread shown in the picture. To make a larger bedspread simply add more strips of motifs until your work reaches the desired size.

Abbreviations
A full list of crochet abbreviations is given on page 26. To work crossed double treble stitches, see page 22.

Working the motif
Make 8ch and join with ss to form a ring.

ROUND 1 12dc into ring, ss into first dc. On all subsequent rounds, work into the back loop of the stitch on the previous round.

ROUND 2 4ch (counts as 1dtr), * 7ch, 1dtr into same st as previous dtr, 1dtr into each of next 3dc; rep from * three times more, omitting dtr at end of last rep, join with ss.

ROUND 3 1dc into dtr, 1dc into each of 3ch, * 2dc into next ch, 1dc into each of 3ch, 1dc into each of 4dtr, 1dc into each of 3ch; rep from * three times more, omitting last dc at end of last rep, ss into first dc.

ROUND 4 4ch (counts as 1dtr), 1dtr into each of next 4dc, * 7ch, 1dtr into each of next 12dc; rep from * three times more, ending last rep 7dtr instead of 12dtr, join with ss.

ROUND 5 1dc into each of 5dtr, 1dc into each of 3ch, * 2dc into next ch, 1dc into each of next 3dc, 1dc into each of next 12dtr, 1dc into each of next 3ch; rep from * three times more, ending last rep 1dc into each of 5dtr, join with ss.

ROUND 6 4ch (counts as 1dtr), 1dtr into each of next 8dc, * 8ch, 1dtr into each of next 20dc; rep from * three times more, ending last rep 11dtr instead of 20dtr, join with ss.

ROUND 7 1dc into each dtr and ch to end, ss into first dc.

ROUND 8 4ch (counts as 1dtr), cross 2dtr, 1dtr into same st as first of the crossed

This beautiful country-style bedspread is worked in a mixture of double crochet and double treble stitches to create contrasting squares in solid and lacy patterns.

dtr, * 3ch, miss 3dc, 1dtr into next dc, cross 2dtr, 1dtr into same st as first of the crossed dtr, 8ch, 1dtr into same st as previous dtr, [cross 2dtr, 1dtr into same st as first of crossed dtr, 3ch, miss 3dc, 1dtr into next dc] twice, cross 2dtr, 1dtr into same st as first of crossed dtr; rep from * twice more, 3ch, miss 3dc, 1dtr into next dc, cross 2dtr, 1dtr into same st as first of crossed dtr, 8ch, 1dtr into same st as previous dtr, rep instructions in brackets, twice, joining with ss instead of last dtr.

ROUND 9 4ch (counts as 1dtr), work 1dtr on each dtr, with crossed dtr and 3ch loops alternating with 8th round, two joined dtr with 8ch at each corner.

ROUND 10 Rep round 9. Fasten off.

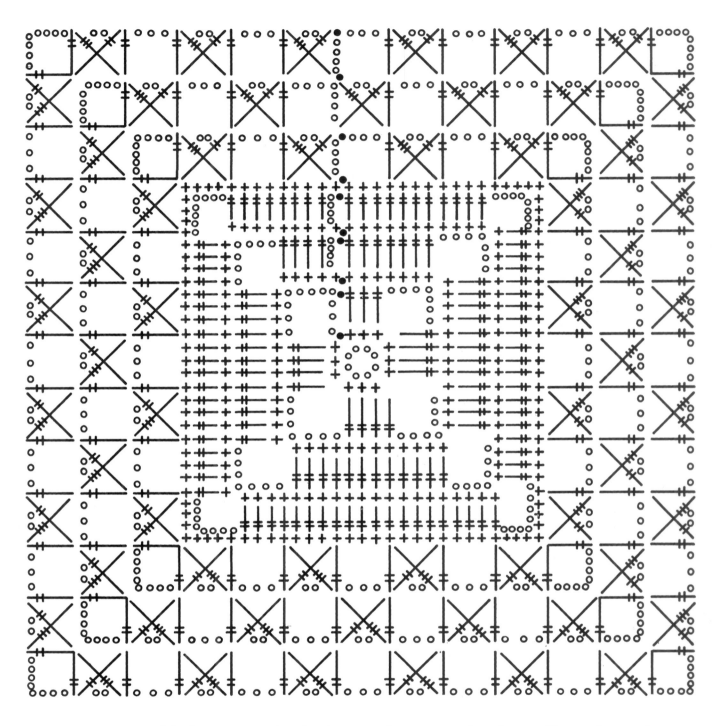

o	ch
●	ss
+	dc
‡	dtr
✕	cross dtrs

Making up the bedspread
1 Sew in the ends. Pin out each motif following the illustrated instructions given on page 30, making sure that all the motifs are of identical size. Spray with water and allow them to dry completely before removing pins.
2 Following the plan above, stitch or crochet the motifs together as shown on page 30. First join seven motifs together to form a strip, then repeat with the remaining motifs until you have nine strips measuring the same length.
3 Join the strips together in the same way to make the completed bedspread. Press on the wrong side using a warm iron.

BUTTERFLY
TABLECLOTH

Worked in filet crochet using fine cotton yarn, this delightful tablecloth features butterfly and rose motifs set within a deep zigzag border. Suitable for the experienced needlewoman, the border will take some time to complete, but the finished tablecloth will give you pleasure for years to come. When not in use, store the tablecloth wrapped in acid-free tissue paper in a cool, dry place.

Materials
White fine crochet cotton, No 40
White cotton or linen fabric
Steel crochet hook 0.6 mm
White sewing thread
Sewing needle
Pins

Measurements
Work sufficient pattern repeats to make a border to fit your table. When buying the fabric, remember to allow a hem allowance of 1.5 cm (⅝ in) all round.

Abbreviations
A full list of crochet abbreviations is given on page 26.
   Special abbreviations for this pattern:
sp(s) = space(s) = two chain, miss two chain or two treble, one treble into next chain or treble
blk(s) = block(s) = four treble (plus three treble for each additional block in group)
   More details of filet crochet are given on page 25.

Working the border
FOUNDATION CHAIN Make 150ch.

ROW 1 1tr into 4th ch from hook, 5tr, 1sp, 3tr, 8sps, 18tr, 2sps, 9tr, 1sp, 6tr, 4sps, 3tr, 17sps, 3tr, turn.

ROW 2 3ch (stands as first tr), 3tr, 16sps, 1blk, 5sps, 5blks, 2sps, 1blk, 4sps, 2blks, 9sps, 1blk, 1sp, 1blk, turn.

Follow chart from third row (arrow on chart shows direction).
When decreasing at the beginning of a row, ss along the top of the blks and when making extension blks at the beginning of a row turn with 8ch; work 1tr into 4th ch from hook and 1tr into each rem ch.
Repeat the 48 pattern rows until the corner is reached, then work only until row 36. Continue straight, turning inside heavy line to top.
Fasten off.
Rejoin yarn at corner arrow.
Work 24 rows along row-ends.

ROW 25 Work across short row then continue along heavy line to inner corner. Continue from chart.

● block

☐ space

After last corner work 14 full width rows.
Fasten off.
Join inner edge of short rows to main border.
Join first and last border rows.

Making up the tablecloth
1 Sew in the ends. Pin out the border a section at a time following the illustrated instructions given on page 30. Spray with water and allow to dry completely before removing the pins.

2 Pin the border on to the fabric to check the fit and carefully cut away any surplus, remembering to leave a 1.5 cm (⅝ in) hem allowance round the edge. Remove the pins and turn a narrow double hem round the cloth and machine stitch or hem neatly by hand. Press the hem well.
3 Pin the border round the cloth, taking care to keep the points evenly spaced along each side. Using small, neat stitches, oversew the crochet border to the fabric. Press lightly on the wrong side with a warm iron.

HEARTS AND DIAMONDS BEDSPREAD

The bedspread is worked in long, narrow strips which are then crocheted together before a narrow border is worked. Make the bedspread in thick, double knitting weight cotton, either in the traditional white, or in a plain colour which coordinates with your bedroom furnishings. Alternatively, use up any oddments of yarn you have and work each strip in a different colour, working the joining stitches and border in either black of white yarn. If you do this, make sure that all the yarns you use are of identical thickness and fibre composition.

Materials
White double knitting weight
  cotton yarn
3.5 mm crochet hook
Tapestry needle size 22 or 24

Measurements
The bedspread is worked in long strips which are about 8 cm (3¼ in) wide. Make sufficient strips to fit the size of your bed, then join the strips together as shown below before working the edging.

Abbreviations
A full list of crochet abbreviations is given on page 26.
  Special abbreviations for this pattern: pct (picot) = three chain, slip stitch in first of these three chain.

A challenging but quite stunning design, this lacy hearts and diamonds pattern is worked in long strips before being crocheted together.

Working the strips
First strip:
Work 27ch.

FOUNDATION ROW Into 4th ch from hook, work 3tr, 2ch, 4tr, 19ch, miss 22ch, [4tr, 2ch, 4tr] into last ch (1 shell made), turn.

ROW 1 (WRONG SIDE) 2ch, shell into first 2ch sp, 19ch, shell into 2ch sp, turn.

ROW 2 Rep row 1.

ROW 3 2ch, shell into first 2ch sp, 9ch, inserting hook under 4 loops work 1dc around the 4 loops together, turn, 3ch (counts as 1tr), 6tr into 9ch sp, turn, * 3ch, 1tr into each of next 6tr, turn; rep from * twice more, 3ch, shell into next 2ch sp, turn.

ROWS 4 TO 7 Rep row 1.

ROW 8 2 ch, shell into first 2ch sp, 9ch, inserting hook under 4 loops insert hook into top of diamond made and work 1dc with 4 loops together, turn, complete diamond as in row 3, 3ch, shell into next 2ch sp, turn.

ROWS 9 TO 12 Rep row 1.

ROW 13 Rep row 8.

Rep from row 4 for the pattern until the strip is the required length, ending with either a 7th or 12th pattern row.

NEXT ROW 2ch, shell into first 2ch sp, 9ch, work 1dc into top of diamond and around 4 loops together, 9ch, shell into next 2ch sp.

Fasten off. Work the remaining strips in the same way.

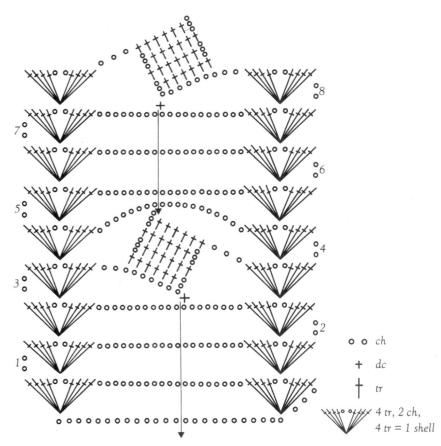

o o *ch*

+ *dc*

† *tr*

4 tr, 2 ch, 4 tr = 1 shell

Joining the strips
With the right side of the work facing, join the yarn in first 2ch turning sp on left-hand strip and work 1dc into this sp, * 4ch, 1dc into next 2ch turning sp on right-hand strip; rep from * until strips are joined.
    Fasten off.
    Repeat to join the rest of strips together.

Working the border
With the right side of the work facing, join yarn in corner 2ch turning sp. Work evenly a border of [2ch, 1dc in edge, pct] along strip to second corner, across the join work 2ch, pct, 2ch, cont in this way ending with [2ch, 1dc in edge, pct] across the last strip to corner, ending 1dc in corner.
    Fasten off.

Finishing off the bedspread
Sew in the ends. Press lightly on the wrong side with a warm iron.

SNOWFLAKE TRAYCLOTH

These quick-to-crochet snowflake motifs are joined together as you work, so the design requires no extra sewing except for finishing off the thread ends on the back. Make the traycloth the right size to fit your tray, then finish off the cloth with a simple two-row edging. By using a heavier white yarn, perhaps double knitting weight cotton, and working more snowflakes this design could also make a lovely, lacy bedspread to decorate a country-style bedroom.

Materials
White fine crochet cotton
2 mm crochet hook
Sewing needle
Pins
Starch (optional)

Measurements
Each motif measures approximately 9 cm (3½ in) across. Work sufficient motifs to cover the base of your tray, joining them together as you work, then work the edging round the outside.

Abbreviations
A full list of crochet abbreviations is given on page 26.

Working the motifs

FIRST SNOWFLAKE
Work 7ch and join with ss to form a ring.

ROUND 1 3ch (counts as 1tr), * 2ch, 1tr into ring; rep from * 10 times more, 2ch, join with ss into 3rd of 3ch. (12 spaced tr).

ROUND 2 3ch (counts as 1tr), * 3ch, 1tr in next tr; rep from * 10 times more, 3ch, join with ss into 3rd of 3ch. (12 spaced tr).

ROUND 3 * Into next loop work 1dc, 1htr, 1tr, 1htr, 1dc (1 shell made); rep from * 11 times more, join with ss into first dc. (12 shells).

ROUND 4 Ss across next htr and into tr at top of shell, * 7 ch, 1dc into tr at centre of next shell; rep from * 10 times more, 7 ch, join with ss into first of 7 ch.

●	ss
o	ch
+	dc
†	htr
╪	tr
■	joining place
⁂	picot

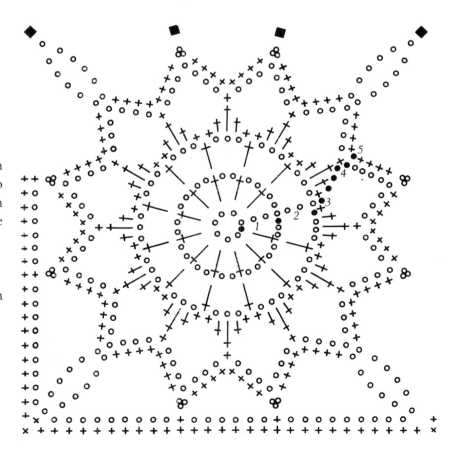

ROUND 5 * Into next loop work 4dc, 11ch, 4dc to form corner, into each of next 2 loops work 4dc, 3ch to form picot, 4dc; rep from * 3 times more, join with ss into first dc.

Fasten off.

SECOND SNOWFLAKE

Work as given above for the first motif until round 4 has been completed, then join second motif to first motif as follows:

ROUND 5 Into first loop of second motif work 4dc, 5ch, place WS of both motifs together and join by working 1dc into 11ch corner loop of first motif, 5ch, return to first loop of second motif, work another 4dc to complete corner, * into next loop work 4dc, 1ch, 1dc into matching picot of first motif, 1ch, 4dc into same loop of second motif, rep from * once more, then into next corner loop of second motif work 4dc, 5ch, 1dc into 11ch corner loop of first motif, 5ch, another 4dc into same loop of second motif to complete corner, work remainder of motif as given for first motif.

Work all further snowflake motifs as given for the second motif, joining the motifs together in the same way as you work. Take care that corner loops are joined with 1dc on the right side whether there are two, three or four corners meeting.

Working the edging
Rejoin the yarn in the first 3ch sp on long edge.

ROW 1 1dc in same sp, * 6ch, 1dc in next 3ch sp, 9ch, 1dc where 11ch loops meet, 9ch; rep from * to end, working

[9ch, 1dc into 11ch loop, 9ch] into single 11ch loop at each corner, join with ss to first dc.

ROW 2 1ch, * 6dc into 6ch loop, 1dc into next dc, 9dc into 9ch loop, 1dc into next dc; rep from * to end, working 3dc

This charming traycloth is crocheted speedily using an attractive snowflake motif. No additional sewing is needed as the motifs are joined together as you work.

into dc at each corner, join with ss into first ch.
Fasten off.

Finishing the traycloth
1 Sew in the ends. Pin out the cloth round the border following the illustrated in-structions given on page 30. Spray with water and allow to dry thoroughly before removing the pins.
2 For a stiffer finish, starch the cloth before pinning it out and finish off by pressing lightly on the wrong side using a warm iron.

SCALLOPED SHELF EDGINGS

These two scalloped edgings are quickly crocheted in thick cotton yarn and they are the perfect way of adding decoration to kitchen or bathroom shelves holding pretty china. Both edgings are worked widthways, so it is easy to make a strip which is just the right length for your shelf. Remember to finish the edging at the end of one complete repeat so that both ends of the strip will match.

White is the classic colour for this type of decoration, but you could work the designs using deep or pastel shades of yarn if you prefer.

Attach the edgings to the shelves with sticky fixing pads so they can be removed easily for laundering.

Materials
White medium-weight No 3 mercerized cotton yarn
3.50 mm crochet hook
Pins

Measurements
Each edging measures approximately 12 cm (4¾ in) deep across the widest point. Each repeat worked will make about 5 cm (2 in) of edging.

Abbreviations
Crochet abbreviations appear on page 26. Special abbreviations for this pattern:
1p = loop

Working the top edging
Work 27ch.

FOUNDATION ROW 1tr into 4th ch from hook, 1tr into each of next 2ch, 2ch, miss 2ch, 1tr into each of next 10ch, 2ch, miss 2ch, 1tr into each of next 7ch, turn.

ROW 1 9ch, ss into 2nd ch from hook and into each of next 3ch, 1tr into each of 8th and 9th ch from hook, (this counts as 3 spare ch for next row, plus 3tr), 1tr into each of next 7tr, 2ch, 1tr into next tr, [2ch, miss 2tr, 1tr into next tr] 3 times, 2ch, 1tr into next tr, 1tr into each of next 2tr, 1tr into top of 3ch, turn.

ROW 2 3ch (counts as first tr), miss 1tr, 1tr into each of next 3tr, [2ch, 1tr into next tr] twice, 2tr into 2ch sp, 1tr into next tr, [2ch, 1tr into next tr] twice, 1tr into each of next 6tr, 2ch, miss 2tr, 1tr into next tr, 1tr into each of the 3 spare ch made on the previous row, turn.

ROW 3 5ch, 1tr into 4th ch from hook, 1tr into next ch, 1tr into next tr, 2ch, miss 2tr, 1tr into next tr, 2tr into next 2ch sp, 1tr into next tr, 2ch, miss 2tr, 1tr into each of next 4tr, 2ch, 1tr into next tr, 2tr into 2ch sp, 1tr into next tr, 2ch, miss 2tr, 1tr into next tr, 2tr into 2ch sp, 1tr into next tr, 2ch, 1tr into each of next 3tr, 1tr in top of 3ch, turn.

ROW 4 3ch, 1tr into each of next 3tr, 2ch, 1tr into next tr, 2ch, miss 2tr, 1tr into next tr, 2tr into 2ch sp, 1tr into next tr, 2ch, miss 2tr, 1tr into next tr, 2ch, 1tr into each of next 4tr, 2tr into 2ch sp, 1tr into next tr, 2ch, miss 2tr, 1tr into next tr, 2tr into 2ch sp, 1tr into next tr, turn.

ROW 5 Ss over first 4tr, 3ch (counts as first tr), 2tr into 2ch sp, 1tr into each of next 7tr, [2ch, 1tr into next tr] twice,

A lovely old-fashioned idea which has recently been revived are these decorative shelf edgings. For those with a little more than basic skills, they make a quick and rewarding project.

2ch, miss 2tr, 1tr into next tr, [2ch, 1tr into next tr] twice, 1tr into each of next 2tr, 1tr in top of 3ch, turn.

ROW 6 3ch, 1tr into each of next 3tr, 2ch, 1tr into next tr, [2tr into 2ch sp, 1tr into next tr] 3 times, 2ch, 1tr into next tr, 1tr into each of next 6tr, turn.

Repeat rows 1 to 6 until the edging is the required length, ending with a 6th row.
Fasten off.

Bottom edging
Work 27ch.

FOUNDATION ROW 1tr into 4th ch from hook, 1tr into each of next 2ch [2ch, miss 2ch, 1tr into each of next 4ch] twice, 2ch, miss 2ch, 1tr into each of next 7ch, turn.

ROW 1 9ch, ss into 2nd ch from hook and into each of next 3ch, 1tr into each of 8th and 9th ch from hook, (this counts as 3 spare ch for next row, plus 3tr), 1tr into each of next 4tr, [2ch, miss 2tr, 1tr into next tr, 2tr into 2ch lp, 1tr into next tr] 3 times, 1tr into each of next 3tr, 1tr into top of 3ch, turn.

ROW 2 3ch (counts as first tr), 1tr into each of next 3tr, [2ch, miss 2tr, 1tr into next tr, 2tr into 2ch lp, 1tr into next tr] twice, 2ch, miss 2tr, 1tr into each of next 4tr, 1tr into each of the 3 spare ch made on the previous row, turn.

ROW 3 5ch, 1tr into 4th ch from hook, 1tr into next ch, 1tr into each of next 4tr, [2ch, miss 2tr, 1tr into next tr, 2tr into 2ch lp, 1tr into next tr] 3 times, 2ch, miss 2tr, 1tr into next tr, 2tr into next 2ch sp, 1tr into each of next 3tr, 1tr into top of 3ch, turn.

ROW 4 3ch (counts as first tr), 1tr into each of next 3tr, [2ch, miss 2tr, 1tr into next tr, 2tr into 2ch lp, 1tr into next tr] 3 times, 2ch, miss 2tr, 1tr into next tr, 2tr into 2ch sp, 1tr into each of next 4tr, turn.

ROW 5 Ss over first 4tr, 3ch (counts as first tr), 1tr into each of next 2tr, 2tr into 2ch sp, 1tr into next tr, [2ch, miss 2tr, 1tr into next tr, 2tr into 2ch lp, 1tr into next tr] 3 times, 1tr into each of next 2tr, 1tr in top of 3ch, turn.

ROW 6 3ch, 1tr into each of next 3tr, [2ch, miss 2tr, 1tr into each of next 4tr] twice, 2ch, miss 2tr, 1tr into each of next 7tr, turn.

Repeat rows 1 to 6 until edging is the required length, ending with a 6th row.
Fasten off.

Finishing the edgings
Pin out each edging in sections following instructions on page 30. Spray with water and allow each section to dry completely before moving on to the next one.

● ss

o ch

† tr

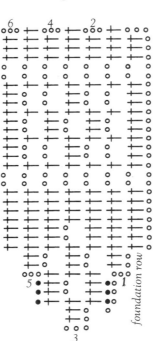

Bottom edging

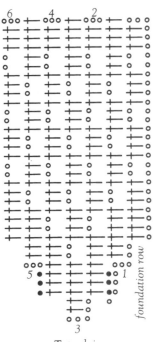

Top edging

ROSES PINCUSHIONS

Two filet crochet rose designs make a pair of useful and ornamental pincushions to keep your pins and needles safe. Backed with white felt and decorated with cotton lace and ribbon trims, either design would make a lovely present for a friend. To make a personalized pincushion, substitute the rose with initials from the alphabet on page 81, centring the letters in a filet crochet rectangle.

Materials (for both designs)
Cream fine crochet cotton
White felt
1.25 mm crochet hook
White ready-frilled cotton lace edging
Cream ready-made ribbon roses
Cream stranded embroidery cotton
Polyester toy stuffing
Tacking cotton
Crewel embroidery needle
Sewing needle
Pins

Measurements
The smaller pincushion measures 11 cm × 12.5 cm (4¼ in × 5 in) minus the edging and the larger one measures 12.5 cm × 15 cm (5 in × 6 in).

Abbreviations
A full list of crochet abbreviations is given on page 26.
Special abbreviations for this pattern:
sp(s) = space(s) (2ch, miss 2ch or 2tr, 1tr into next ch or tr)
blk(s) = block(s) (4tr, plus 3tr for each additional block in group)

More details of how to work filet crochet are given on page 25.

Large pincushion
FOUNDATION CHAIN Make 60 ch.

ROW 1 1tr into 4th ch from hook, 1tr into each ch across row.
(58tr)

ROW 2 3ch (counts as 1tr), 1tr into next 3tr, 6sps, 2blks, 9sps, 1blk, turn.
Follow the chart from the third row until the complete design has been worked.
Fasten off.

Small pincushion
FOUNDATION CHAIN Make 52ch.
ROW 1 1tr into 4th ch from hook, 1tr into each ch across row.

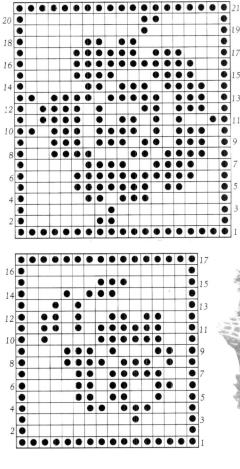

● block
☐ space

ROW 2 3ch (counts as 1tr), 1tr into next 3tr, 14sps, 1blk, turn.

Follow the chart from the third row until the design is complete.
Fasten off.

Making up the pincushions
Both designs are made up as follows:
1 Sew in the ends. Pin out the rose motif following the illustrated instructions given on page 30. Spray with water and allow the crochet to dry completely before removing the pins.
2 Pin the crochet on to the felt and cut round the edge leaving a margin of at least 2.5 cm (1 in) all round. Cut out a second piece of felt to the same size. Tack the lace edging to the wrong side of the crochet, neatly turning under the raw ends.
3 Place the backing felt on a flat surface. Cover with the other piece, then place the lace-trimmed crochet right side upwards on top. Tack all the layers together.
4 Using three strands of embroidery thread and beginning at the centre of one of the long sides, stitch through the layers close to the edge of the crochet. Use double running stitch and make sure you catch the lace edging with the stitching. Leave an opening of about 5 cm (2 in) along the last side and do not break off the thread.
5 Remove the tacking stitches which are holding the layers together, but not those securing the lace edging. Stuff the pincushion carefully with polyester stuffing, using the point of the crochet hook to help you gently manoeuvre the stuffing right into the corners.
6 Using the attached thread, complete the outside row of stitching and fasten off securely. Remove the tacking stitches from the lace. Turn the pincushion over and carefully trim away the surplus felt round the edge. Sew a ribbon rose in each corner of the crocheted square design.

Pretty little pincushions display two quick-to-work rose motifs. Decorated with little ribbon roses and lace edging, they make ideal gifts.

CROCHET BAGS

Crochet bags are fun to work and they are useful in many ways around the home. The two bags shown here hold soap and bathroom accessories and could be hung on the back of the door or looped on to a towel rail. Worked in other colours of yarn, the bags would be perfect for daytime or evening wear, accommodating purse, keys, handkerchief, makeup bag – and even a paperback novel – with ease, while the same bag worked in sturdy string would be useful for carrying shopping home.

Materials
Cream double knitting weight cotton or
 ribbon yarn
3.5 mm crochet hook
Tapestry needle

Measurements
Each bag measures approximately 19 cm (7½ in) round the widest part and 28 cm (11 in) from top to the centre of the base.

Abbreviations
A full list of crochet abbreviations is given on page 26.

COTTON YARN BAG

Working the bag
Work 6ch and join with ss to form a ring.

ROUND 1 5ch, * 2tr into ring, 2ch, rep from * 4 times more, 1tr into ring, ss to 3rd of first 5ch.

ROUND 2 Ss into 2ch sp, 5ch, 1tr into same sp, * 1tr into each of next 2tr, [1tr, 2ch, 1tr] into 2ch sp; rep from * 4 times more, 1tr into each of next 2tr, ss to 3rd of 5ch.

ROUND 3 Ss into 2ch sp, 5ch, 1tr into same sp, * 1tr into each of next 4tr, [1tr, 2ch, 1tr] into 2ch sp; rep from * 4 times more, 1tr into each of next 4tr, ss to 3rd of first 5ch.

ROUNDS 4 AND 5 Work 2 more rounds in the same way, working 2 more tr along each side each time.

ROUND 6 Ss into 2ch sp, 5ch, * miss 1tr, 1tr into each of next 8tr, 2ch, 1tr into 2ch sp, 2ch; rep from * to end, but omit last 1tr and 2ch and ss to 3rd of 5ch.

ROUND 7 Ss into 2ch sp, 5ch, * work tr2tog, 1tr into each of next 4tr, tr2tog, 2ch, [1tr into 2ch sp, 2ch] twice; rep from * 5 times more, but omit last 1tr and 2ch and ss to 3rd of first 5ch.

ROUND 8 Ss into 2ch sp, 5ch, * work tr2tog, 1tr into each of next 2tr, tr2tog, 2ch, 1tr into 2ch sp, 2ch, 3tr into 2ch sp, 2ch, 1tr into 2ch sp, 2ch; rep from * 5 times more but omit last tr and 2ch and ss to 3rd of first 5ch.

ROUND 9 Ss over 2ch sp and into next tr, 3ch, 1tr into each of next 3tr, * 2ch, miss next 2ch sp, 1tr into next 2ch sp, 1tr into each of next 3tr, 1tr into next 2ch sp, miss next 2ch sp, 1tr into each of next 4tr; rep from * 5 times more but omit last 4tr and ss to 3rd of first 3ch.

ROUND 10 Ss into next tr, 3ch, 1tr into next tr, * 2ch, 1tr into 2ch sp, 1tr into each of next 5tr, 1tr into 2ch sp, 2ch, miss 1tr, 1tr into each of next 2tr; rep

The basic pattern for these lovely little bags can easily be adjusted to make other types: an evening purse perhaps or even a shopping holdall.

from * 5 times more but omit last 2tr and ss to 3rd of first 3ch.

ROUND 11 3ch, 1tr into next tr, * 3tr into 2ch sp, 1tr into each of next 7tr, 3tr into 2ch sp, 1tr into each of next 2tr; rep from * 5 times more but omit last 2tr and ss to 3rd of first 3ch. (90tr)

ROUND 12 3ch, tr2tog, * 3 ch, tr3tog; rep from * 28 times more, 3ch, ss to top of first group of tr.

ROUND 13 Ss to centre of 3ch sp, 4ch, * 1dc into next 3ch sp, 3ch; rep from * to end, ss to first of first 4ch.

ROUND 14 Ss to centre of first 3ch sp, 3ch, 2tr into same sp, 3tr into each 3ch sp all round, ss into 3rd of first 3ch. (90tr)

ROUND 15 4ch, * miss next tr, 1tr into next tr, 1ch; rep from * to end, ss into 3rd of first 4ch.

ROUND 16 Ss into 1ch sp, 4ch, * 1tr into next 1ch sp, 1ch; rep from * to end, ss to 3rd of first 4ch.

ROUNDS 17, 18 AND 19 Rep round 16 3 times more.

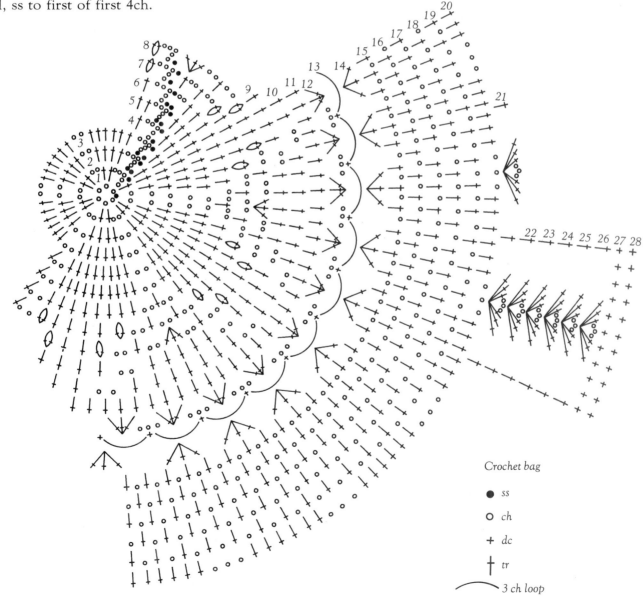

Crochet bag

● *ss*

○ *ch*

+ *dc*

† *tr*

⌒ *3 ch loop*

ROUND 20 3ch, [1tr into 1ch sp, 1tr into next tr] twice, 1tr into 1ch sp, * 3ch, miss 3sts, 1tr into each of next 6 sts; rep from * 8 times more, 3ch, miss 3 sts, ss to 3rd of first 3ch.

ROUND 21 Ss over next 2tr, 3ch, * [3tr, 3ch, 3tr] into 3ch sp, 1tr between 3rd and 4th tr of 6tr; rep from * 8 times more, [3tr, 3ch, 3tr] into 3ch sp, ss to 3rd of first 3ch.

ROUND 22 3ch, * [3tr, 3ch, 3tr] into 3ch sp, 1tr into single tr; rep from * 8 times more, [3tr, 3ch, 3tr] into 3ch sp, ss to 3rd of first 3ch.

ROUNDS 23, 24, 25 AND 26 Rep round 22 4 times more.

ROUND 27 1ch, 1dc into next 3tr, * 3dc into 3ch sp, 1dc into next 7tr; rep from * to end, ss into first dc.

ROUND 28 1ch, 1dc into each dc on previous round, ss into first dc. Fasten off.

RIBBON YARN BAG
Work 6ch and join with a ss to form a ring.

ROUND 1 5ch, * 2tr into ring, 2ch; rep from * 4 times more, 1tr into ring, ss to 3rd of first 5ch.

ROUND 2 Ss into 2ch sp, 5ch, 1tr into same sp, * 1tr into each of next 2tr, [1tr, 2ch, 1tr] into 2ch sp; rep from * 4 times more, 1tr into each of next 2tr, ss to 3rd of 5ch.

ROUND 3 Ss into 2ch sp, 5ch, 1tr into same sp, * 1tr into each of next 4tr, [1tr, 2ch, 1tr] into 2ch sp; rep from * 4 times more, 1tr into each of next 4tr, ss to 3rd of first 5ch.

ROUNDS 4 AND 5 Work 2 more rounds in the same way, working 2 more tr along each side each time.

ROUND 6 Ss into 2ch sp, 5ch, * miss 1tr, 1tr into each of next 8tr, 2ch, 1tr into 2ch sp, 2ch; rep from * to end, but omit last 1tr and 2ch and ss to 3rd of 5ch.

ROUND 7 Ss into 2ch sp, 5ch, * work tr2tog, 1tr into each of next 4tr, tr2tog, 2ch, [1tr into 2ch sp, 2ch] twice; rep

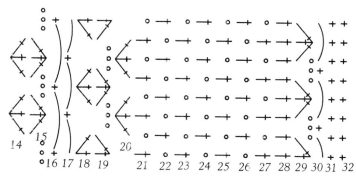

Ribbon bag

1st to 14th rows alike for both bags

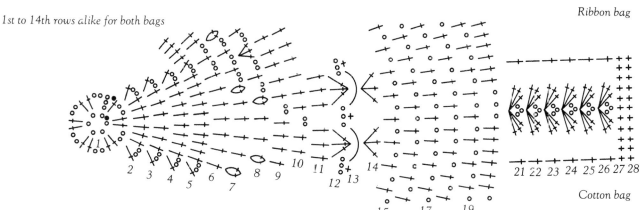

Cotton bag

from * 5 times more, but omit last 1tr and 2ch and ss to 3rd of first 5ch.

ROUND 8 Ss into 2ch sp, 5ch, * work tr2tog, 1tr into each of next 2tr, tr2tog, 2ch, 1tr into 2ch sp, 2ch, 3tr into 2ch sp, 2ch, 1tr into 2ch sp, 2ch; rep from * 5 times more but omit last tr and 2ch and ss to 3rd of first 5ch.

ROUND 9 Ss over 2ch sp and into next tr, 3ch, 1tr into each of next 3tr, * 2ch, miss next 2ch sp, 1tr into next 2ch sp, 1tr into each of next 3tr, 1tr into next 2ch sp, miss next 2ch sp, 1tr into each of next 4tr; rep from * 5 times more but omit last 4tr and ss to 3rd of first 3ch.

ROUND 10 Ss into next tr, 3ch, 1tr into next tr, * 2ch, 1tr into 2ch sp, 1tr into each of next 5tr, 1tr into 2ch sp, 2ch, miss 1tr, 1tr into each of next 2tr; rep from * 5 times more but omit last 2tr and ss to 3rd of first 3ch.

ROUND 11 3ch, 1tr into next tr, * 3tr into 2ch sp, 1tr into each of next 7tr, 3tr into 2ch sp, 1tr into each of next 2tr; rep from * 5 times more but omit last 2tr and ss to 3rd of first 3ch. (90tr)

ROUND 12 3ch, work tr2tog, * 3ch, tr3tog; rep from * 28 times more, 3ch, ss to top of first group of tr.

ROUND 13 Ss to centre of 3ch sp, 4ch, * 1dc into next 3ch sp, 3ch; rep from * to end, ss to first of first 4ch.

ROUND 14 Ss to centre of first 3ch sp, 3ch, 2tr into same sp, 3tr into each 3ch sp all round, ss to 3rd of first 3ch. (90tr)

ROUNDS 15 AND 18 Rep round 12.

ROUNDS 16 AND 19 Rep round 13.

ROUNDS 17 AND 20 Rep round 14.

ROUND 21 4ch, * miss next tr, 1tr into next tr, 1ch; rep from * to end, ss to 3rd of first 4ch.

ROUND 22 Ss into 1ch sp, 4ch, * 1tr into next 1ch sp, 1ch; rep from * to end, ss to 3rd of first 4ch.

ROUNDS 23, 24, 25, 26 AND 27 Rep round 22.

ROUND 28 3ch, 1tr into next ch sp, * 1tr into next tr, 1tr into ch sp; rep from * to end, ss to 3rd of 3ch. (90tr)

ROUND 29 Rep round 12.

ROUND 30 Rep round 13.

ROUND 31 Ss into next 3ch sp, 1ch, 2dc into first 3ch sp, * 3dc into next 3ch sp; rep from * to end, ss to ch.

ROUND 32 1ch, 1dc into each dc on previous round, ss into first dc. Fasten off.

Making the cords

Cut 12 lengths of yarn, each 120 cm (47 in) long. Plait 6 lengths for each cord, knotting the ends to leave a group of threads about 8 cm (3 in) long at each end.

Making up the bags

Sew in the ends. Press cotton yarn lightly on the wrong side if necessary, but do not press ribbon yarn. Thread one cord through the row of holes along the top of the bag then thread the second cord through the same holes so the loose ends emerge on the opposite side of the bag. Knot each pair of loose ends together about 1 cm (½ in) above the existing knots.

LAVENDER BAGS

Delicate crochet hexagons worked in
fine white cotton are backed with a
contrasting colour felt to make a
pair of delightful lavender bags. Felt
does not fray in use, so a decorative
edge is quickly made by cutting the
felt margin round the crochet with a
pair of pinking shears.

Materials
White fine cotton yarn
Contrasting felt
1.25 mm crochet hook
Stranded cotton to match felt
Crewel embroidery needle
Sewing needle
Tacking thread
Pins
Dried lavender

Measurements
Each sachet measures about 12 cm (4¾ in).

*Dried lavender has been
used for centuries, not
only to keep stored linen
and lingerie sweet-
smelling, but also to
ward off moths. Fill
these simple-to-crochet
sachets with a handful
as a gift or for your own
use.*

Abbreviations
A full list of crochet abbreviations is given on page 26.

WINDMILL HEXAGON
Work 5ch and join with ss to form a ring.
ROUND 1 * 6ch, 1dc into ring; rep from * 5 times more, ss over first 3ch of first 6ch lp.

ROUND 2 * 4ch, 1dc into 6ch lp; rep from * 5 times more, working last dc into ss before 4 ch.

ROUND 3 * 4ch, 2dc into 4ch lp, 1dc into dc; rep from * 5 times more, working last dc into last dc at end of round 2.

ROUND 4 * 4ch, 2dc into 4ch lp, 1dc into each of next 2dc; rep from * to end.

ROUND 5 * 4ch, 2dc into 4ch lp, 1dc into each of next 3dc; rep from * to end.

Cont in this way, working 1 more dc in each group on each round until there are 9dc in each group.

ROUND 10 * 4ch, 2tr into 4ch lp, 1tr into each of next 8dc; rep from * to end.

ROUND 11 * 4ch, 2tr into 4ch lp, 1tr into each of next 9tr; rep from * to end.

ROUND 12 Ss into first ch of 4ch lp, 1ch, * [2dc, 3ch, 2dc] into 4ch lp, 1dc into each tr along side; rep from * to end, join with ss into 1ch.

ROUND 13 3ch, 1tr into next dc, * [2tr, 3ch, 2tr] into 3ch sp, 1tr into each tr along side; rep from * to end, ss into 3rd of 3ch.

ROUND 14 1ch, 1dc into next tr, * 5dc into 3ch sp, 1dc into each tr along side; rep from * to end, ss into 1ch.
Fasten off.

FLOWER HEXAGON
Work 6ch. Join with ss to form ring.
ROUND 1 4ch, [1tr into ring, 1ch] 11 times, join with ss to 3rd of 4ch.

ROUND 2 3ch, 2tr into sp, 1tr into tr, 2ch, * 1tr into tr, 2tr into sp, 1tr into tr, 2ch; rep from * 4 times more, join with ss to 3rd of 3ch.

ROUND 3 3ch, 1tr into same place, 1tr into each of next 2tr, 2tr into next tr, 2ch, * 2tr into next tr, 1tr into each of next 2tr, 2tr into next tr, 2ch; rep from * 4 times, join with ss to 3rd of 3ch.

ROUND 4 3ch, 1tr into same place, 1tr into each of next 4tr, 2tr into next tr, 2ch, * 2 tr into next tr, 1tr into each of next 4tr, 2tr into next tr, 2ch; rep from * 4 times, join with ss to 3rd of 3ch.

ROUND 5 3ch, 1tr into each of next 7tr, * 3ch, 1dc into 2ch sp, 3ch, 1tr into each of next 8tr; rep from * 4 times more, 3ch, 1dc into 2ch sp, 3ch, join with ss to 3rd of 3ch.

ROUND 6 Ss into next tr, 3ch, 1tr into each of next 5tr, * 3ch, [1dc into 3ch sp, 3ch] twice, miss next tr, 1 tr into each of next 6tr; rep from * 4 times more, 3ch, [1dc into 3ch sp, 3ch] twice, join with ss to 3rd of 3ch.

ROUND 7 Ss into next tr, 3ch, 1tr into each of next 3tr, * 3ch, [1dc into 3ch sp, 3ch] 3 times, miss next tr, 1tr into each of next 4tr; rep from * 4 times more, 3ch, [1dc into 3ch sp, 3ch] 3 times, join with ss to 3rd of 3ch.

ROUND 8 Ss between 2nd and 3rd tr of group, 3ch, 1tr into same place, * 3ch, [1dc into 3ch sp, 3ch] 4 times, 2tr between 2nd and 3rd tr of group; rep from * 4 times more, 3ch, [1dc into 3ch sp, 3ch] 4 times, join with ss to 3rd of 3ch.

ROUND 9 Ss into 3ch sp, 3ch, 3tr into same sp, [4tr into 3ch sp] 4 times, * 3ch, miss 2tr, [4tr into 3ch sp] 5 times; rep from * 4 times more, 3 ch, join with ss to 3rd of 3ch.

ROUND 10 1ch, * 1dc into each tr along edge, 5dc into 3ch sp; rep from * 5 times more, join with ss to first ch. Fasten off.

Making up the bags

1 Sew in the ends. Pin out the hexagon motif following the illustrated instructions given on page 30. Spray with water and allow to dry thoroughly before removing the pins.
2 Pin the motif on to the felt and cut round the edge leaving a margin of at least 2.5 cm (1 in) all round. Cut out a second piece of felt to the same size.
3 Place the backing felt on a flat surface. Cover with the other piece, then centre the crochet motif on top, right side up. Tack all the layers together.
4 Using three strands of embroidery thread and beginning about 1 cm (½ in) to the right of the first corner, stitch through all the layers close to the edge of the crochet using double running stitch. Leave an opening of about 2.5 cm (1 in) along the last side and do not break off the thread.
5 Remove the tacking and fill the bag with dried lavender. Using the attached thread, close up the opening and fasten off the edges securely.
6 Finally trim away the surplus felt about 6 mm (¼ in) from the edge of the crochet using pinking shears.

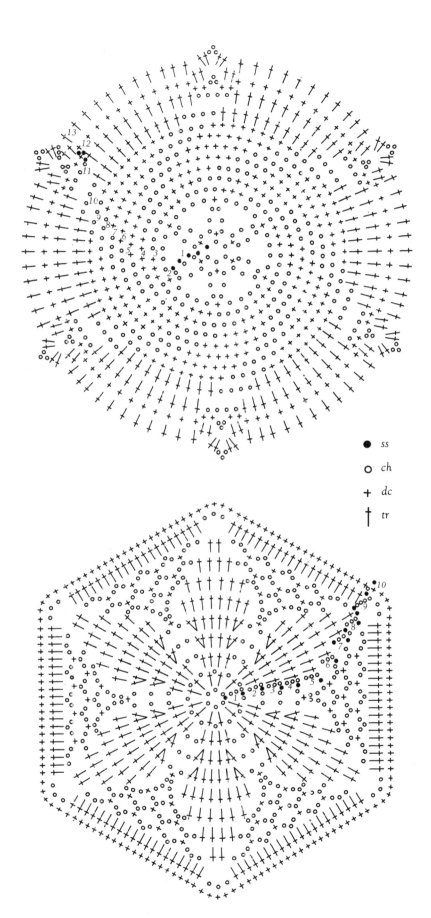

● ss
○ ch
+ dc
† tr

CHRISTMAS
STARS

Tiny, five-pointed crochet stars make such pretty Christmas tree decorations. Work the pattern in fine cotton, then dip the stars into a solution of stiff-finish starch or PVA craft medium (white craft glue) diluted with cold water. Make sure you let each star dry thoroughly after pinning it out to shape, then remove the pins, thread narrow ribbon through one of the points and hang the star on the tree. You could also work this design in fine gold or silver yarn.

Materials
White crochet cotton size 10
1 mm crochet hook
Red narrow satin ribbon
Stiff-finish starch or PVA craft medium
Tapestry needle size 22 or 24
Pins

Measurements
Each star measures approximately 9 cm (3½ in) across. You can make larger stars by working the same pattern using a thicker yarn and larger hook.

Abbreviations
A full list of crochet abbreviations is given on page 26.

Working the stars
Centre (make 1):
Work 5ch and join with ss to form a ring.

ROUND 1 3ch, 1tr into ring, [2ch, 2tr into ring] 4 times more, 2ch, ss to 3rd of 3ch.

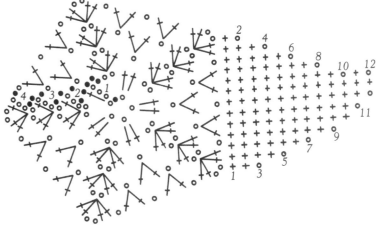

The perfect project for a beginner, these delightful little stars look wonderful against the deep green foliage of the traditional Christmas tree. If you only want to make a few, try working them in gold or silver yarn to highlight your tree.

ROUND 4 Ss into next 2ch sp, work beg shell into same sp, [1ch, 2tr into next 1ch sp] twice, 1ch, [shell into next 2ch sp, 1ch, 2tr into next 1ch sp, 1ch, 2tr into next 1ch sp, 1ch] 4 times, ss to 3rd of 3ch.
Fasten off.

Points (make 5):
ROW 1 Rejoin yarn in any 2ch space of shell, 1ch, 1dc into same sp, [1dc into each of next 2tr and ch sp] 4 times, 1ch, turn.
(13dc)

ROW 2 Miss first dc, work dc across row, 1ch, turn.
(12dc).

ROWS 3 TO 11 Rep row 2, missing first dc at beg of every row to decrease 1st.
(3dc rem at end of row 11)

ROW 12 1dc into 2nd dc, ss into next dc.
Fasten off.

To work subsequent star points, rejoin yarn in same 2ch sp where row 1 of previous point began and rep rows 1 to 12 to complete each point.

Finishing off the stars
1 Sew in the ends. Starch the stars stiffly following the manufacturer's instructions or dip each one into a solution of PVA (white craft glue) and water. Pin out the stars following the illustrated instructions given on page 30 and allow them to dry completely before removing the pins.
2 Thread a length of narrow red ribbon through the tip of one point on each star and tie it to form a hanging loop.

● *ss*

○ *ch*

+ *dc*

† *tr*

⚓ *1 shell*

ROUND 2 Ss into next 2ch sp, 3ch, 1tr into same space, 2ch, 2tr into same sp (beg shell made), 1ch, into next 2ch sp work 2tr, 2ch, 2tr (shell made), [1ch, 1 shell into next 2ch sp] 3 times more, 1ch, join with ss to 3rd of 3ch.

ROUND 3 Ss into next 2ch sp, work beg shell into same sp, 1ch, 2tr into next 1ch sp, 1ch, [shell into next 2ch sp, 1ch, 2tr into next 1ch sp, 1ch] 4 times, ss to 3rd of 3ch.

Pattern Library

CROCHET EDGINGS

Here are four different crochet edgings to try. Work the cream or green edging in fine cotton with a small hook – the finished effect will be narrow and delicate, perfect for lingerie. The peach and beige edgings are substantial enough to edge a traycloth or small tablecloth.

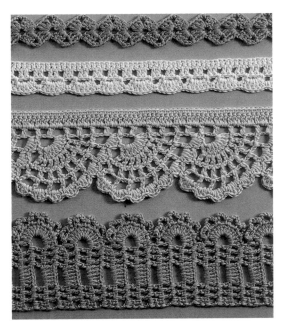

Abbreviations
Crochet abbreviations appear on page 26.

INTERWOVEN CROCHET BRAID (green)
Work 3ch.
FOUNDATION ROW Work * 3tr, 3ch, 3tr, 3ch, * into 2nd ch from hook, turn.
ROW 1 Rep from * to * into 3ch sp of previous row, turn.
Repeat row 1.

NARROW SHELLS (cream)
Work a multiple of 6ch plus 3.
FOUNDATION ROW Work 1dc into 2nd ch from hook, 1dc into each ch to end, turn.
ROW 1 3ch, miss first dc, 1tr into next dc, * 1ch, miss 1dc, 1tr into each of next 2dc; rep from * to end, turn.

ROW 2 5ch, 1dc into next ch sp, * 4ch, 1dc into next ch sp; rep from * to last 2 sts, 2ch, 1tr into 3rd of 3ch, turn.
ROW 3 1ch, 1dc into first tr, * 5tr into next 4ch sp, 1dc into next 4ch sp; rep from * to end, working last dc into 3rd of 5ch.

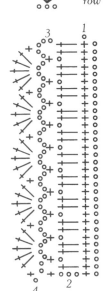

Foundation row

● ss
○ ch
+ dc
† tr

SCALLOPED EDGING (peach)

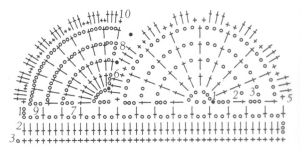

Work 8ch and join with ss; form ring.
ROW 1 3ch, 8tr into ring, turn.
ROW 2 4ch, 1tr into next tr, * 1ch, 1tr into next tr; rep from * 5 times more, 1ch, 1tr into 3rd of 3ch.
ROW 3 5ch, 1tr into next tr, * 2 ch, 1tr into next tr; rep from * 5 times more, 2ch, 1tr into 3rd of 4ch.
ROW 4 6ch, 1tr into next tr, * 3ch, 1tr into next tr; rep from * 5 times more, 3ch, 1tr into 3rd of 5ch.
ROW 5 * [1dc, 3tr, 1dc] into 3ch sp; rep from * 7 times more, 8ch, turn and ss into 2nd of first 3tr, turn.
ROW 6 3ch, 1tr into 8ch lp, turn.
ROW 7 4ch, 1tr into next tr, * 1ch, 1tr into next tr; rep from * 5 times more, 1ch, 1tr into 3rd of 3ch, ss into 2nd tr of next group of 3tr, turn.
ROW 8 5ch, miss first tr, 1tr into next tr; rep row 3 from * to end, turn.
ROW 9 Rep row 4, then ss into 2nd tr of next group of 3tr, turn.
Repeat rows 5 to 9, finishing with a 5th row, but omitting the 8ch at the end of the row.

Heading:

ROW 1 Working along top straight edge of scalloped edging, work 5ch, 1tr into next row-end, * 2ch, 1tr into next row-end; rep from * to end, turn.

ROW 2 3ch, * 2tr into 2ch sp, 1tr into next tr; rep from * to end, working last tr into 3rd of 5ch.

ROW 3 1ch, * 1dc into each tr; rep from * to end, working last dc into 3rd of 3ch. Fasten off.

EDWARDIAN FENCE EDGING (beige)

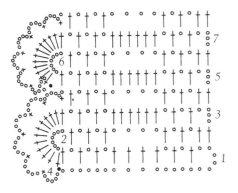

Work 20ch.

ROW 1 Work 1tr into 7th ch from hook, [1ch, miss 1ch, 1tr into next ch], twice, 2tr into each of next 2ch, [1tr into next ch, 1ch, miss 1ch] 3 times, 1tr into last st, 7ch, turn.

ROW 2 1tr into first 1ch sp, [1ch, 1tr into next 1ch sp] twice, 4ch, [1tr into next 1ch sp, 1ch] twice, 1tr into top of turning ch, 1tr into next ch, 4ch, turn.

ROW 3 [1tr into next 1ch sp, 1ch] twice, 6tr into 4ch lp, [1ch, 1tr into next 1ch sp] twice, 1ch, 12tr into 7ch lp at end of row and secure with a ss into last st of foundation ch, 5ch, turn.

ROW 4 1dc into 2nd st, [5ch, miss 1st, 1dc into next st] 5 times, 1ch, [1tr into next 1ch sp, 1ch] twice, 1tr into next 1ch sp, 4ch, [1tr into next 1ch sp, 1ch] twice, 1tr into first st of turning ch, 1tr into next st, 4ch, turn.

ROW 5 [1tr into next 1ch sp, 1ch] twice, 6tr into 4ch lp, 1ch, [1tr into next 1ch sp, 1ch] twice, 1tr into first of 5ch, 7ch, turn.

ROW 6 Rep row 2.

ROW 7 Rep row 3, but after working the 12tr group, work a ss into the st of 5ch close to the tr previously worked.

ROW 8 Rep row 4.

Repeat rows 5 to 8.

CROCHET BORDERS

The two deep crochet borders take their inspiration from traditional Irish crochet patterns. Suitable for edging a wide variety of household articles – from towels to pillowcases, either border can also be used as a shelf edging. For a more delicate result, try working the border designs in a fine mercerized crochet cotton using a small hook.

Abbreviations

Crochet abbreviations appear on page 26.

SHAMROCK BORDER (blue)

Work 21ch.

FOUNDATION ROW 1tr into 8th ch from hook, [2ch, miss 2ch, 1tr into next ch] 3 times, 5ch, miss 3ch, [1tr, 3ch] 3 times into next ch, 1tr into same ch, 1ch, turn.

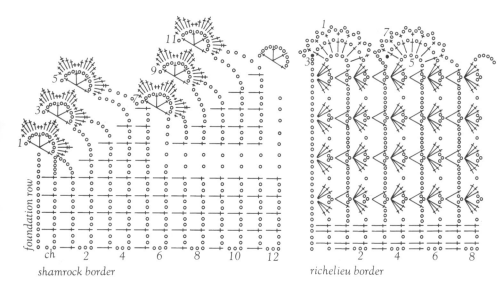

shamrock border

richelieu border

o   ch

+   dc

†   htr

†   tr

‡   dtr

●   ss

ROW 1 [1dc, 1htr, 1tr, 1dtr, 1tr, 1htr, 1dc] into each of next three 3ch sps (shamrock made), 5ch, 1tr into 5ch lp (on future repeats, this will be a 7ch lp), [2ch, 1tr into next tr] 4 times, 2ch, miss 2ch, 1tr into next ch, 5ch, turn.

ROW 2 1tr into next tr, [2ch, 1tr into next tr] 4 times, 2ch, 1tr into 5ch lp, 7ch, [1tr, 3ch] 3 times into dtr at centre of second petal, 1tr into same place, 1ch, turn.

ROW 3 Make shamrock as before, 5ch, 1tr into 7ch lp, * 2ch, 1tr into next tr; rep from * to end, working last tr into 3rd of 5ch, 5ch, turn.

ROW 4 Rep row 2, but work [2ch, 1tr into next tr] 6 times instead of 4 times.

ROW 5 Rep row 3.

ROW 6 1tr into next tr, [2ch, 1tr into next tr] 3 times, 7ch, miss 4sps, [1tr, 3ch] 3 times into next sp, 1tr into same sp, 1ch, turn.

Repeat rows 1 to 6, ending with a 5th row.

RICHELIEU BORDER *(peach)*

Work 35ch.

FOUNDATION ROW 1tr into 3rd ch from hook, 1ch, miss 1ch, 1tr into each of next 2ch, 1ch, miss 3ch, 3tr into next

ch, 3ch, 3tr into next ch, [1ch, miss 5ch, 3tr into next ch, 3ch, 3tr into next ch] 3 times, leave last 3ch unworked, 6ch, turn.

ROW 1 [1tr, 3ch, 1tr] into 3ch lp, [5ch, (1tr, 3ch, 1tr) into next 3ch lp] 3 times, 3ch, 1tr into each of next 2tr, 1ch, 1tr into last tr, 1tr into 3rd of 6ch, 3ch, turn.

ROW 2 1tr into next tr, 1ch, 1tr into each of next 2tr, [1ch, (3tr, 3ch, 3tr) into 3ch lp] 4 times, [1ch, 1tr] 7 times into 3ch lp, ss to last ch of foundation row.

* Note that in future repeats, the ss at the end of row 2 is worked into the 3ch lp of the previous pattern.

ROW 3 [3ch, 1dc into 1ch sp] 7 times, 3ch, [1tr, 3ch, 1tr] into 3ch sp, [5ch, (1tr, 3ch, 1tr) into next 3ch lp] 3 times, 3ch, 1tr into each of next 2tr, 1ch, 1tr into next tr, 1tr into turning ch, 3ch, turn.

ROW 4 1tr into next tr, 1ch, 1tr into each of next 2tr, [1ch (3tr, 3ch, 3tr) into 3ch lp] 4 times, 6ch, turn.

Repeat rows 1 to 4.

SQUARE CROCHET MOTIFS

Abbreviations

Crochet abbreviations appear on page 26.

Special abbreviation for Afghan square: 1cl (1 cluster) = ** yarn round hook (yrh), insert hook into ring, yarn round hook, draw loop through, yarn round hook, draw loop through 2 loops **, repeat from ** to ** 3 times more, yarn round hook, draw loop through 4 loops.

OLD AMERICA *(mauve and white)*

Using light coloured yarn, work 6ch and join with ss to form a ring.

ROUND 1 (Light) 3ch (counts as 1tr), 2tr into ring, 3ch, * 3tr into ring, 3ch; rep

into each corner sp; cont from * to end, ending with 1ch, ss into 3rd of 3ch. Break off yarn.

ROUND 4 (Dark) Join yarn to corner sp, 3ch, [2tr, 3ch, 3tr] into same sp, * 1ch, 3tr into each 1ch sp, 1ch, [3tr, 3ch, 3tr] into each corner sp; cont from * to end, ending with 1ch, ss into 3rd of 3ch. Break off yarn.

AFGHAN SQUARE (beige)

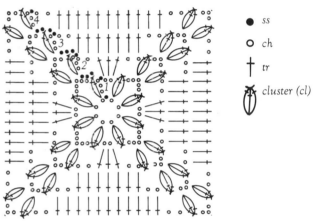

Work 8ch; join with ss to form ring.
ROUND 1 3ch, ** yrh, insert hook into ring, yrh, draw lp through, yrh, draw through 2 lps **, rep from ** to **, yrh, draw through 3lps, 5ch. * 1cl, 2ch, 1cl, 5ch; rep from * twice more, 1cl, 2ch, join with ss into 3rd of 3ch.
ROUND 2 Ss into 5ch sp, 3ch, rep from ** to ** twice, yrh, draw through 3lps, 2ch, 1cl into same sp, * 2ch, 3tr into 2ch sp, 2ch, [1cl, 2ch, 1cl] into 5ch sp, rep from * twice more, 2ch, 3tr into 2ch sp, 2ch, join with ss to 3rd of 3ch.
ROUND 3 Ss into corner 2ch sp, 3ch, rep from ** to ** twice, yrh, draw through 3lps, 2ch, 1cl into same sp, * 2ch, 2tr into 2ch sp, 1tr into each of next 3tr, 2tr into 2ch sp, 2ch, [1cl, 2ch, 1cl] into corner 2ch sp, rep from * twice more, 2ch, 2tr into 2ch sp, 1tr into each of next 3tr, 2tr into 2ch sp, 2ch, join with ss to 3rd of 3ch.

Square crochet motifs are internationally popular, from the traditional Old America design (shown here in mauve and white) to the modern Afghan square (see the beige example).
All the designs can be worked in several colours, by simply breaking off the yarn at the end of each round and joining in another colour, but they look equally effective worked in a single colour.

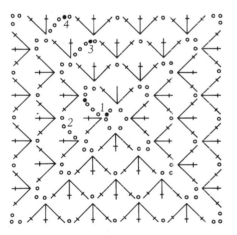

from * twice more, ss into 3rd of 3ch. Break off yarn.

ROUND 2 (Dark) Join yarn to 3ch sp, 3ch, [2tr, 3ch, 3tr] into same sp, * 1ch, [3tr, 3ch, 3tr] into next 3ch sp; rep from * twice more, ss into 3rd of 3ch. Break yarn.

ROUND 3 (Light) Join yarn to corner sp, 3ch, [2tr, 3ch, 3tr] into same sp, * 1ch, 3tr into each 1ch sp, 1ch, [3tr, 3ch, 3tr]

ROUND 4 Rep round 3, but working 1tr into each of 7tr instead of 3tr along each side.

Cont in this way, working 4 more tr along each side in each round until square is required size.
Fasten off.

FRAMED SUN (green)

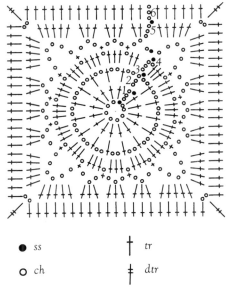

●	*ss*	†	*tr*
○	*ch*	‡	*dtr*

Work 8ch; join with ss to form ring.

ROUND 1 3ch (counts as 1tr), work 15tr into ring, ss to 3rd of 3ch.

ROUND 2 5ch (counts as 1tr, 2ch), [1tr into next tr, 2ch] 15 times, ss to 3rd of 5ch.

ROUND 3 3ch, 2tr into first sp, 1ch, [3tr, 1ch] into each sp, ss to 3rd of 3ch.

ROUND 4 * [3ch, 1dc into next 1ch sp] 3 times, 6ch, 1dc into next sp; cont from * to end, ss to first of 3ch.

ROUND 5 3ch, 2tr into first 3ch sp, 3tr into each of next two 3ch sps, * [5tr, 2ch, 5tr] into each corner sp, 3tr into each 3ch sp; cont from * to end, join with ss to 3rd of 3ch.

ROUND 6 3ch, work 1tr into each st and [1tr, 1dtr, 1tr] into each 2ch corner sp.
Fasten off.

ST GEORGE SQUARE (peach)

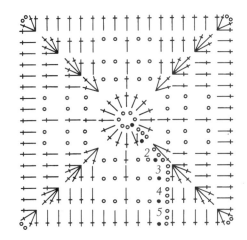

Work 6ch. Join with ss to form ring.
ROUND 1 3ch (counts as 1tr), work 15tr into ring, join with ss into 3rd of 3ch.
ROUND 2 3ch (counts as 1tr), 2tr into same st as last ss, 2ch, miss 1tr, 1tr into next tr, 2ch, miss 1tr, * 3tr into next tr, 2ch, miss 1tr, 1tr into next tr, 2ch, miss 1tr; rep from * twice, join with ss into 3rd of 3ch.
ROUND 3 3ch, 5tr into next tr, * 1tr into next tr, [2ch, 1tr into next tr] twice, 5tr into next tr; rep from * twice, [1tr into next tr, 2ch] twice, join with ss into 3rd of 3ch.
ROUND 4 3ch, 1tr into each of next 2tr, 5tr into next tr, * 1tr into each of next 3tr, 2ch, 1tr into next tr, 2ch, 1tr into each of next 3tr, 5tr into next tr; rep from * twice, 1tr into each of next 3tr, 2ch, 1tr into next tr, 2ch, join with ss into 3rd of 3ch.
ROUND 5 3ch, 1tr into each of next 4tr, [2tr, 2ch, 2tr] into next tr, * 1tr into each of next 5tr, 2tr into next 2ch sp, 1tr into next tr, 2tr into next 2ch sp, 1tr into each of next 5tr, [2tr, 2ch, 2tr] into next tr; rep from * twice, 1tr into each of next 5tr, 2tr into next 2ch sp, 1tr into next tr, 2tr into last ch sp, join with ss to 3rd of 3ch. Fasten off.

HEXAGONAL CROCHET MOTIFS

Abbreviations

Crochet abbreviations appear on page 26. Special abbrev. for popcorn motif:

popcorn = work 5 trebles into next stitch, drop loop from hook, insert hook into top of first of these trebles, pick up dropped loop and draw through, work 1 chain to secure popcorn.

picot = work 3 chain then work slip stitch into first of these chain.

CLEMATIS HEXAGON (cream)

Work 6ch. Join with ss to form ring.

ROUND 1 1ch, 12dc into ring, ss to first dc.
ROUND 2 1ch, 1dc into same place as 1ch, [7ch, miss 1dc, 1dc into next dc] 5 times, 3ch, miss 1dc, 1dtr into top of first dc.
ROUND 3 3ch (counts as 1tr), 4tr into lp formed by dtr, [3ch, 5tr into next 7ch lp] 5 times, 3ch, ss into 3rd of 3ch.
ROUND 4 3ch (counts as 1tr), 1tr into each of next 4tr, * 3ch, 1dc into next 3ch sp, 3ch **, 1tr into each of next 5tr; rep from * 4 times more and then from * to ** once again, ss to 3rd of 3ch.
ROUND 5 3ch, tr4tog over next 4tr (counts as tr5tog), * [5ch, 1dc into next 3ch sp] twice, 5ch **, tr5tog over next 5tr; rep from * 4 times and then from * to ** once again, ss into top of tr4tog.
ROUND 6 Ss into each of next 3ch, 1ch, 1dc into same place, * 5ch, 1dc into next 5ch sp; rep from * to end, omitting last dc and ending with ss into first dc.
ROUND 7 Ss into each of next 3ch, 1ch, 1dc into same place, * 5ch, 1dc into next 5ch sp, 3ch, [5tr, 3ch, 5tr] into next sp, 3ch, 1dc into next sp; rep from * 5 more times, omitting last dc and ending with ss into first dc.
Fasten off.

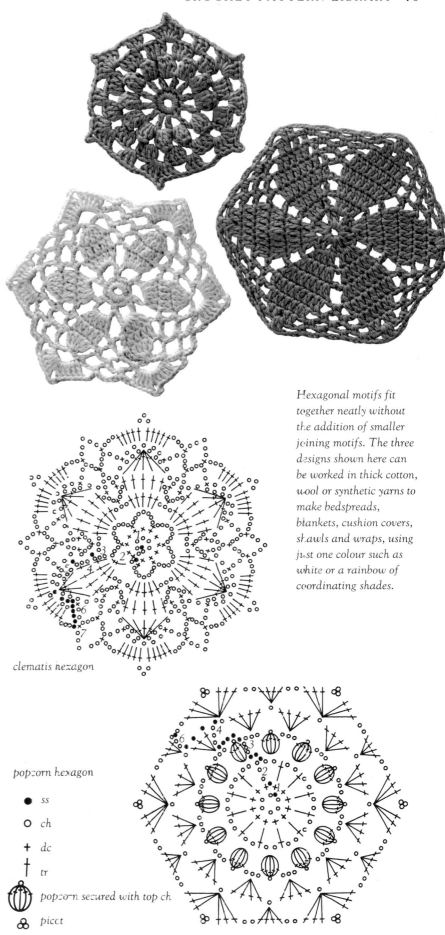

Hexagonal motifs fit together neatly without the addition of smaller joining motifs. The three designs shown here can be worked in thick cotton, wool or synthetic yarns to make bedspreads, blankets, cushion covers, shawls and wraps, using just one colour such as white or a rainbow of coordinating shades.

clematis hexagon

popcorn hexagon

● ss
○ ch
+ dc
† tr
popcorn secured with top ch
picot

FLOWER HEXAGON (*mauve*)

Work 6ch. Join with ss to form a ring.

ROUND 1 4ch (counts as 1tr, 1ch), [1tr into ring, 1ch] 11 times, join with ss to 3rd of 4ch.

ROUND 2 3ch (counts as 1tr), 2tr into 1ch sp, 1tr into next tr, 2ch, * 1tr into next tr, 2tr into 1ch sp, 1tr into next tr, 2ch; rep from * 4 times more, join with ss to 3rd of 3ch.

ROUND 3 3ch, 1tr into same place, 1tr into each of next 2tr, 2tr into next tr, 2ch, * 2tr into next tr, 1tr into each of next 2tr, 2tr into next tr, 2ch; rep from * 4 times, join with ss to 3rd of 3ch.

ROUND 4 3ch, 1tr into same place, 1tr into each of next 4tr, 2tr into next tr, 2ch, * 2tr into next tr, 1tr into each of next 4tr, 2tr into next tr, 2ch; rep from *4 times more, join with ss to 3rd of 3ch.

ROUND 5 3ch, 1tr into each of next 7tr, * 3ch, 1 dc into 2ch sp, 3ch, 1tr into each of next 8tr; rep from * 4 times more, 3ch, 1dc into 2ch sp, 3ch, join with ss to 3rd of 3ch.

ROUND 6 Ss into next tr, 3ch, 1tr into each of next 5tr, * 3ch, [1dc into 3ch sp, 3ch] twice, miss next tr, 1tr into each of next 6tr; rep from * 4 times more, 3ch, [1dc into 3ch sp, 3ch] twice, join with ss to 3rd of 3ch.

ROUND 7 Ss into next tr, 3ch, 1tr into each of next 3tr, * 3ch, [1dc into 3ch sp, 3ch] 3 times, miss next tr, 1tr into each of next 4tr; rep from * 4 times more, 3ch, [1 dc into 3ch sp, 3ch] 3 times, join with ss to 3rd of 3ch.

ROUND 8 Ss between 2nd and 3rd tr of group, 3ch (counts as 1tr), 1tr into same place, * 3ch, [1dc into 3ch sp, 3ch] 4 times, 2tr between 2nd and 3rd tr of group; rep from * 4 times more, 3ch, [1dc into 3ch sp, 3ch] 4 times, join with ss to 3rd of 3ch.
Fasten off.

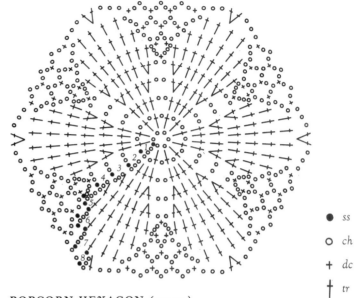

●	*ss*
○	*ch*
+	*dc*
✝	*tr*

POPCORN HEXAGON (*green*)

Work 6ch and join with ss to form a ring.

ROUND 1 1ch, work 12dc into ring, join with ss into first dc.

ROUND 2 5ch (counts as 1tr, 2ch), miss first dc, [1tr into next dc, 2ch] 11 times, join with ss into 3rd of 5ch.

ROUND 3 Ss into first 2ch sp, 3ch, 4tr into same sp as ss, drop loop from hook, insert hook into top of 3ch, pick up dropped loop and draw through, 1ch to secure (counts as first popcorn), 3ch, [1 popcorn into next 2ch sp, 3ch] 11 times, join with ss into top of first popcorn.

ROUND 4 Ss into first 3ch sp, 3ch (counts as 1tr), 3tr into same sp as ss, 1ch, [4tr into next 3ch sp, 1ch] 11 times, join with ss to 3rd of 3ch.

ROUND 5 Ss into each of next 3tr and into next ch sp, 3ch, 3tr into same sp as last ss, 2ch, [3tr, 1 picot, 3tr] into next ch sp, * 2ch, 4tr into next ch sp, 2ch, [3tr, 1 picot, 3tr] into next ch sp; rep from * 4 times more, 2ch, join with ss to 3rd of 3ch.
Fasten off.

CIRCULAR CROCHET MOTIFS

Abbreviations
Crochet abbreviations appear on page 26.

TINY ROSE (blue)

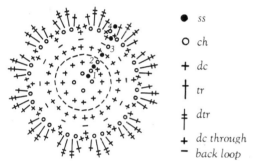

- ● ss
- ○ ch
- + dc
- † tr
- ‡ dtr
- + dc through back loop

Work 4ch. Join with ss to form ring.

ROUND 1 1ch, 12dc into ring, join with ss to first ch.
ROUND 2 1ch, 2dc into each dc (inserting hook into back loop of each st), join with ss to first ch.
ROUND 3 1ch, * 1dc into next dc (inserting hook into back loop of st), 2ch, miss 1dc; rep from * to end, join with ss to first ch.
ROUND 4 1ch, * [1dc, 1tr, 2dtr, 1tr, 1dc] into next 2ch sp; rep from * to end, join with ss to first ch. Fasten off.

ELIZABETHAN FLOWER (pink)
Work 8ch. Join with ss to form a ring.

ROUND 1 6ch (counts as 1tr, 3ch), [1tr into ring, 3ch] 7 times, join with ss to 3rd of 6ch.
ROUND 2 3ch (counts as 1tr), 5tr into first 3ch sp, [6tr into next 3ch sp] 7 times, join with ss to 3rd of 3ch.
ROUND 3 3ch, 1tr into each of next 5tr (inserting hook into back loop of each st), 3ch, [1tr into each of next 6tr (inserting hook into back loop of each st), 3ch] 7 times, join with ss to 3rd of 3ch.

- ● ss
- ○ ch
- + dc
- † tr
- + dc through back loop
- † dc around previous three rounds 6ch lps

ROUND 4 4ch (counts as 1dtr), 1dtr into each of next 5tr leaving last lp of each dtr on hook (6 loops on hook), [yrh, pull through 3 lps] twice, yrh, pull through 2 lps, 8ch, 1dc into 3ch sp, 8ch, * 1dtr into each of next 6tr leaving last lp on hook (7 lps on hook), [yrh, pull through 3 lps] 3 times, 8ch, 1dc into 3ch sp, 8ch; rep from * 6 times more, join with ss to top of first dtr group.
ROUND 5 [9dc into next 8ch sp] 16 times, join with ss to first dc. Fasten off.

Work small motifs, such as the tiny rose shown in blue, in fine, metallic yarn. One motif could decorate a knitted garment, or several could hang on a Christmas tree.
Larger designs, like the snowflake circle, can be worked in thick cotton yarn and used on its own as a mat to protect a polished table top.

SNOWFLAKE CIRCLE *(peach)*

Work 10ch and join with ss to form a ring.

ROUND 1 24dc into ring, ss into first dc.

ROUND 2 [6ch, miss 2dc, 1dc into next dc] 8 times, ss into first ch.

ROUND 3 [8dc into next 6ch sp] 8 times, ss into first dc.

ROUND 4 5ch (counts as 1tr, 2ch), miss 1dc, * 1tr into back loop of next dc, 2ch, miss 1dc; rep from * to end, ss into 3rd of 5ch.

ROUND 5 [2dc into next 2ch sp] to end, ss into first dc.
(64dc)

ROUND 6 1dc into back loop of each dc to end, ss into first dc.

ROUND 7 Working into both loops of each st, [2dc into next dc, 1dc into next dc] to end.
(96dc)

ROUND 8 Rep round 6.

ROUND 9 Rep round 4.

ROUND 10 Ss into next 2ch sp, 3ch (counts as 1tr), 1tr into same sp, 2ch, 2tr into same sp, * 6ch, miss two 2ch sps, [2tr, 2ch, 2tr] into next 2ch sp; rep from * ending 6ch, ss into 3rd of 3ch.
(16tr groups)

ROUND 11 Ss into next 2ch sp, 3ch (counts as 1tr), 1tr into same sp, 2ch, 2tr into same sp, 6ch, * [2tr, 2ch, 2tr] into next 2ch sp, 6ch; rep from * to end, ss into 3rd of 3ch.

ROUND 12 Rep round 11.

ROUND 13 Ss into next 2ch sp, 3ch, 1tr into same sp, 2ch, 2tr into same sp, 4ch, insert hook under three 6ch lps of previous 3 rounds and work 1dc to enclose ch lps, 4ch, * [2tr, 2ch, 2tr] into next 2ch sp, 4ch, 1dc to enclose ch lps as before, 4ch; rep from * to end, ss into 3rd of 3ch.
Fasten off.

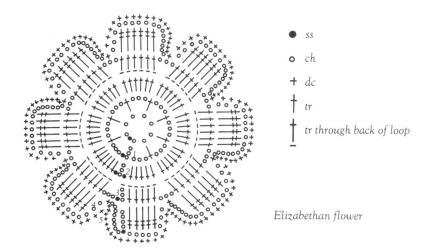

●	ss
○	ch
+	dc
†	tr
⊥	tr through back of loop

Elizabethan flower

OPENWORK PATTERNS

Abbreviations

Crochet abbreviations appear on page 26.

Abbreviation for lattice stripes: puff st = [yarn over hook, draw through a loop] 3 times, yarn over hook and draw through all 7 loops on hook, 1 chain to finish.

SHADOWS AND SPACES *(blue)*

Work a multiple of 6ch plus 3.

FOUNDATION ROW Work 1tr into 4th ch from hook, 1tr into each ch to end, 3ch, turn.

ROW 1 1tr into next st, * 3ch, miss 3 sts, 1tr into each of next 3 sts; rep from * to

Three of the patterns, shown in cream, pink and beige, are perfect for working in fine two and three ply wool or synthetic yarns to make light, summery wraps and square shawls. The fourth pattern, shown in blue, is best worked in fine or medium-weight cotton yarn and would make an unusual café-style curtain.

end, ending with 1tr into last st, 1tr into top of turning ch, turn.

ROW 2 * 3tr into 3ch sp, 3ch; rep from * to end, ending with 1ch, 1tr into top of turning ch, 3ch, turn.

ROW 3 1tr into 1ch sp, * 3ch, 3tr into 3ch sp; rep from * to end, ending with 2tr into turning ch, 3ch, turn.

ROW 4 1tr into each ch and st to end of row, 3ch, turn.

ROW 5 1tr into each st to end, 3ch, turn.

ROW 6 Rep row 5.

Repeat rows 1 to 6.

BAR AND LATTICE (beige)

Work a multiple of 4ch plus 6.

FOUNDATION ROW 1tr into 10th ch from hook, * 3ch, miss 3ch, 1tr into next ch; rep from * to end, 4ch, turn.

ROW 1 * 1dc into 2nd of 3ch, 2ch, 1tr into next tr, 2ch; rep from * to end, ending with 1dc into 2nd ch, 2ch, 1tr into turning ch, 5ch, turn.

ROW 2 1tr into next tr, * 3ch, 1tr into next tr; rep from * to end, working last tr into turning ch, 4ch, turn.

Repeat rows 1 and 2.

FANCY TRELLIS (cream)

Work a multiple of 4ch plus 6.

FOUNDATION ROW Work [1dc, 3ch, 1dc] into 6th ch from hook, * 5ch, miss 3ch, [1dc, 3ch, 1dc] into next ch; rep from * to end, ending with 1dc into last ch, 5ch, turn.

ROW 1 * [1dc, 3ch, 1dc] into 3rd ch of 5ch lp, 5ch; rep from * to end, ending with 5ch, 1dc into turning ch, 5ch, turn.

Repeat row 1.

LATTICE STRIPES (pink)

Work a multiple of 8ch plus 2.

FOUNDATION ROW Work 1dc into 2nd ch from hook, * 2ch, miss 3ch, [1tr, 3ch, 1tr] into next ch, 2ch, miss 3ch, 1dc into next ch; rep from * to end, 6ch, turn.

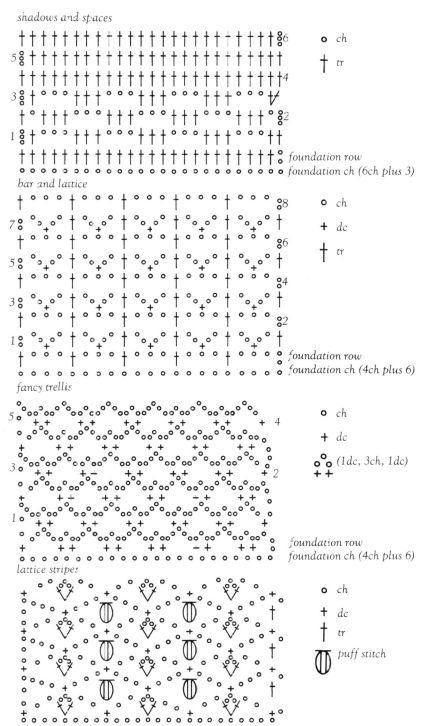

shadows and spaces

o ch
† tr

foundation row
foundation ch (6ch plus 3)

bar and lattice

o ch
+ dc
† tr

foundation row
foundation ch (4ch plus 6)

fancy trellis

o ch
+ dc
oo (1dc, 3ch, 1dc)
++

foundation row
foundation ch (4ch plus 6)

lattice stripes

o ch
+ dc
† tr
puff stitch

ROW 1 * 1dc into 3ch lp, 3ch, 1 puff st into dc, 3ch; rep from * to end, ending with 1tr into last dc, 1ch, turn.

ROW 2 1dc into first st, * 2ch, [1tr, 3ch, 1tr] into next dc, 2ch, 1dc into top of puff st; rep from * to end, ending with 1dc into turning ch, 6ch, turn.

Repeat rows 1 and 2.

SHELL STITCHES

Abbreviations
Crochet abbreviations appear on page 26.

LARGE SHELLS (cream)

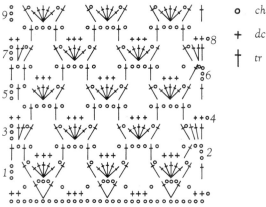

foundation ch (10ch plus 2)

Work a multiple of 10ch plus 2.
FOUNDATION ROW Work 1dc into first ch from hook, 1dc into next ch, * 1ch, miss 3ch, [1tr, 3ch, 1tr] into next ch, 1ch, miss 3ch, 1dc into each of next 3ch; rep from * to end, ending with 1dc into each of last 2ch, 3ch, turn.
ROW 1 * 1tr into first tr, 1ch, 5tr into 3ch sp, 1ch, 1tr into last tr of group; rep from * to end, ending with 1tr into last st, 4ch, turn.
ROW 2 * 1tr into first tr of group, 1ch, 1dc into each of centre 3 sts, 1ch, 1tr into last tr of group, 3ch; rep from * to end, ending with 1ch, 1tr into turning ch, 3ch, turn.
ROW 3 2tr into 1ch sp, 1ch, 1tr into next st, * 1tr into first tr of next group, 1ch, 5tr into 3ch sp, 1ch, 1tr into last tr of group; rep from * to end, ending with 1tr into last tr, 1ch, 3tr into turning ch, 1ch, turn.
ROW 4 1dc into first st, 1dc into next st, 1ch, 1tr into next tr, * 3ch, 1tr into first tr of group, 1ch, 1dc into each of centre 3 sts, 1ch, 1tr into last st of group; rep from * to end, ending with 1dc into last st, 1dc into turning ch, 3ch, turn.
Repeat rows 1 to 4.

VENETIAN SHELLS (green)

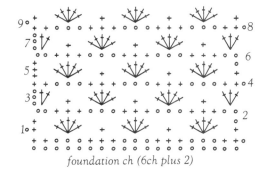

foundation ch (6ch plus 2)

Work a multiple of 6ch plus 2.

FOUNDATION ROW 1dc into 2nd ch from hook, 1dc into next ch, * 3ch, miss 3ch, 1dc into each of next 3ch; rep from * to last 5ch, 3ch, miss 3ch, 1dc into each of last 2ch, 1ch, turn.
ROW 1 1dc into first dc, * 5tr into 3ch sp, miss 1dc, 1dc into next dc; rep from * to end, 3ch, turn.
ROW 2 * 1dc into 2nd, 3rd and 4th of 5tr group, 3ch; rep from * to end, ending with 1dc into 2nd, 3rd and 4th of 5tr

Shell stitches are quick and easy to work and create a very attractive result whether the shells are arranged in vertical rows, as in the beige example, or alternately, like the green example. Work shell stitches in fine, soft yarns to make lacy shawls, and baby clothes, or in heavier weight wool or cotton for household items.

group, 2ch, 1dc into last st, 3ch, turn.
ROW 3 2tr into 2ch sp, miss 1dc, 1dc into
next dc, * 5tr into 3ch sp, miss 1dc, 1dc
into next dc; rep from * to end, 3tr into
last ch sp, 1ch, turn.
ROW 4 1dc into each of first 2tr, * 3ch,
1dc into 2nd, 3rd and 4th of 5tr group;
rep from * to end, ending with 3ch, 1dc
into each of last 2tr, 1ch, turn.
Repeat rows 1 to 4.

SHELL STRIPES (beige)

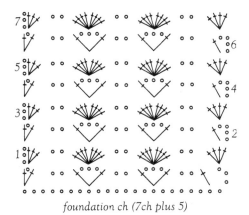

foundation ch (7ch plus 5)

Work a multiple of 7ch plus 5.
FOUNDATION ROW Work 1tr into 5th ch
from hook, * 2ch, miss 6ch, [1tr, 3ch,
1tr] into next ch; rep from * to end,
ending with [1tr, 1ch, 1tr] into last ch,
3ch, turn.
ROW 1 3tr into 1ch sp, * 8tr into 3ch sp;
rep from * to end, ending with 5tr into
turning ch, 4ch, turn.
ROW 2 1tr into first st, * 2ch, [1tr, 3ch,
1tr] into space between 4th and 5th sts
of group; rep from * to end, ending [1tr,
1ch, 1tr] into last st, 3ch, turn.
Repeat rows 1 and 2.

TINY SHELLS (pink)

Work a multiple of 6ch plus 4.
FOUNDATION ROW [1tr, 2ch, 1tr] into 7th
ch from hook, * miss 2ch, [2tr, 1ch, 2tr]
into next ch, miss 2ch, [1tr, 2ch, 1tr]
into next ch; rep from * to last 3ch,
miss 2ch, 1tr into last ch, 3ch, turn.

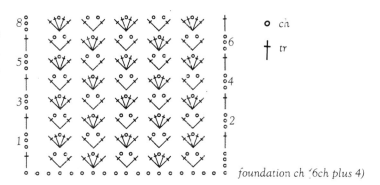

foundation ch (6ch plus 4)

o ch

† tr

ROW 1 * [2tr, 1ch, 1tr] into 2ch sp, [1tr,
2ch, 1tr] into 1ch sp; rep from * to end,
ending with [2tr, 1ch, 2tr] into 2ch sp,
1tr into turning ch, 3ch, turn.
ROW 2 * [1tr, 2ch, 1tr] into 1ch sp, [2tr,
1ch, 2tr] into 2ch sp; rep from * to end,
ending with [1tr, 2ch, 1tr] into 1ch sp,
1tr into turning ch, 3ch, turn.
Repeat rows 1 and 2.

FILET CROCHET
MOTIFS

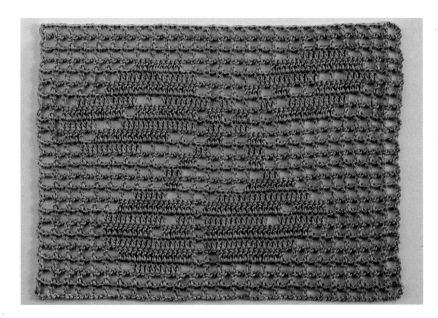

These pictorial charts can be used in a
variety of ways. Small motifs worked in
fine yarn make pincushions and sachets.
Other designs can be worked in thicker
cotton for cushion covers or tablemats.

As well as altering the size, different yarns will affect the final appearance – fine yarns give a lacy look, while heavy yarns produce a more substantial piece.

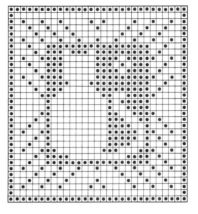

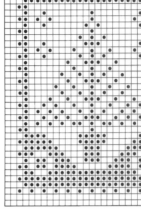

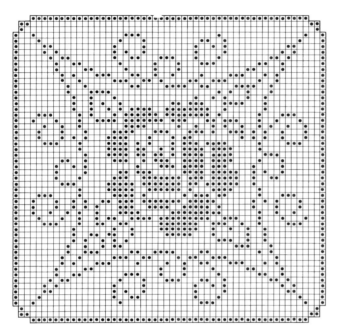

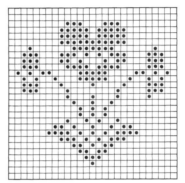

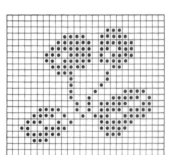

FILET CROCHET INSERTIONS AND BORDERS

This selection of charts for filet crochet insertions and borders gives you pictorial designs and abstract designs. All are worked widthways which means you simply work at a strip until it is the right length for your needs, remembering to finish working at the end of a repeat, so the pattern at both ends of the strip will match.

Use insertions between two pieces of fabric to decorate tablecloths or bedlinen, while the borders can edge anything.

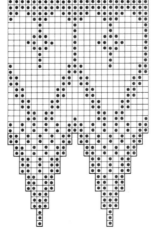

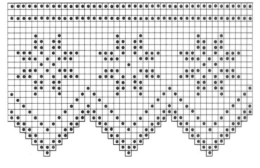

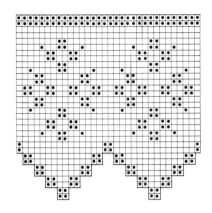

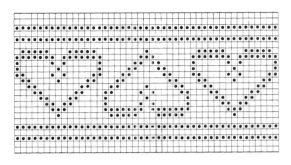

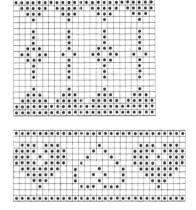

FILET CROCHET ALPHABET

This alphabet can be used to decorate many crochet items from personalized borders for bath towels, to larger pieces such as cushion covers and pictures which spell out a name or greeting.

First work out your designs on graph paper, then work up a small sample piece before beginning on the complete project. You will find full instructions on page 25 showing how to make your own chart and how to work from a chart.

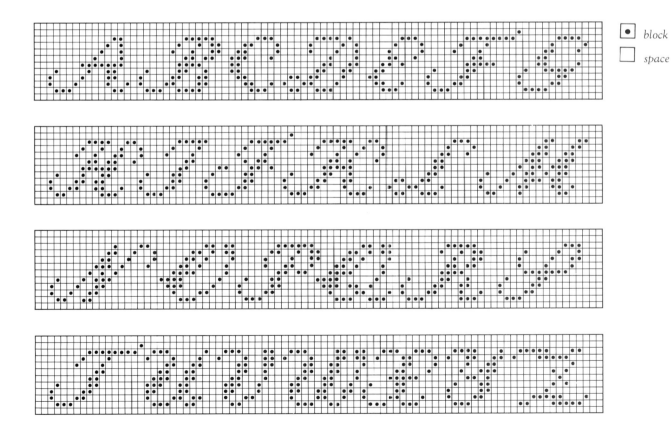

● block
☐ space

The craft of knitting

Knitting dates back to the seventh century and has a long and distinguished history. From the patterned table carpets of the European knitting guilds to fine Elizabethan stockings and the wonderfully intricate shawls still made in the Shetland Isles, knitting skills have spread throughout much of the world. In recent times, knitting has been one of the most popular pastimes for both women and men, with a wealth of yarns and patterns available to whet even the most jaded appetite.

Many people knit sweaters, scarves and baby clothes, but few modern knitters are familiar with the beauty of lace made in this way. Whether worked in rows or rounds, a piece of knitted lace can be as fine, light and delicate as a cobweb or thick and soft with an interesting texture. The difference depends not only on the stitch pattern being used, but also on your choice of yarn and needles.

A LOOK BACK IN TIME

Knitting is the craft of making a looped fabric from a continuous length of yarn using two or more eyeless needles. The fabric can be flat or tubular. The craft has a long history with the earliest known pieces – discovered in parts of the Middle East – dating back to the seventh century. Textile fragments excavated from earlier cultures, Peruvian (900 BC to AD 600) and Coptic (4th century AD), were thought to show examples of knitting, but extensive studies of the fabrics have shown that the fragments were not constructed from one continuous piece of yarn. Instead, separate lengths were used, looped together using a needle with an eye.

The fragments of knitting which date from the seventh century show evidence of great skill and technical proficiency on the part of the workers – the pieces are knitted with coloured yarn in sophisticated geometric patterns which reflect contemporary tile and carpet designs. Although there is no hard evidence to allow us to trace the spread of knitting accurately from these early beginnings, it is safe to assume that knitting was brought by traders, sailors and soldiers from the Middle East to Europe.

The earliest reference to knitting in Europe is in a fourteenth century painting by Master Bertram. The painting, called 'The Visit of Angels', is part of the Buxtehude altarpiece and shows the Virgin Mary picking up stitches on a knitted shirt using four double-pointed needles. The name 'knitting' is taken from the Anglo-Saxon word *cnittan*, meaning threads woven by hand.

By the mid sixteenth century, the craft of knitting had spread widely throughout Europe and the first knitting guild was formed in Paris in 1527. Guilds were almost exclusively a male preserve – women had the tedious task of spinning the yarn, then it was knitted up by men, a much more skilled and therefore prestigious occupation. Widows were the only women allowed to enter guild membership, providing their husband had been a guild member and they could cope with their dead husband's entire workload themselves. Guilds promoted a very high standard of craftsmanship with apprentices having to work and study for six years before knitting and preparing a shirt, a pair of socks, a felted cap and a colourwork carpet for their final examination.

As knitting guilds spread through Europe, different countries became renowned for making particular types of garments. France, Spain and Italy produced delicate, lacy silk gloves, stockings and jackets, while in southern Europe most knitting was worked into church vestments and ornaments. By contrast, in Germany and Austria, the majority of knitting was worked in wool yarn and the knitted fabric was usually heavily embroidered. This region became famous for making large knitted table carpets which were also used as luxurious wall hangings. The carpets were worked on a knitting frame instead of needles. The frames were set with pegs round which various colours of yarn were wound to make loops. The loops were then slipped off the pegs to create a knitted fabric. Although this technique had virtually died out by the mid nineteenth century, it still survives today in the form of the colourful tubes of bobbin or 'French' knitting made by children.

In England, knitted stockings became fashionable after Queen Elizabeth I accepted a pair of knitted silk stockings as a New Year's gift in 1560. This period heralded the beginning of knitting as both a flourishing domestic craft and a cottage industry, particularly as wool production was an important part of the country's economy.

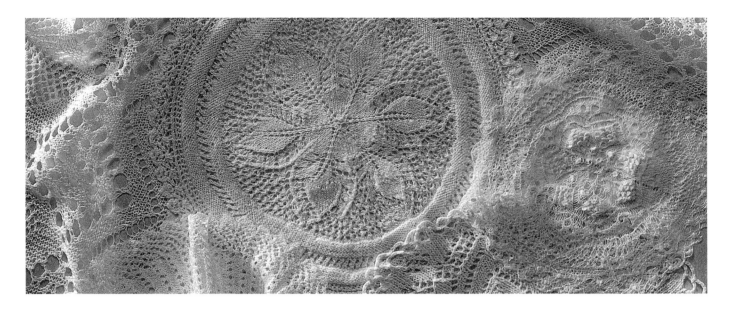

EARLY KNITTING NEEDLES

The earliest knitting needles were made from a variety of materials including wood, copper, bone, metal wire, ivory and tortoiseshell and they became prized possessions. Needles were referred to by various terms during the sixteenth century, frequently they were called 'wires' or 'pins', particularly in Essex. The inventory of a Durham mercer, John Farbeck, dated 20 November 1597 refers to them as 'knitting pricks'; while an Italian dictionary compiled and published by John Florio in 1598 gives the first recorded mention of 'knitting needles'.

Needles were often made by the knitters themselves. The points were kept sharp by regularly regrinding and they were carefully protected with wooden or cork stoppers. When not in use, knitting needles were wrapped in leather folders or stored in cases or carved wood or ivory.

Knitting sheaths or sticks were used to speed up the work – essential for those knitting for a living. The sheaths, often beautifully carved and decorated, were tucked into the knitter's belt or apron strings on the right hip. The sheath held the end of the right-hand needle firmly, leaving the right hand free to knit, moving the stitches rapidly from needle to needle. As many as 200 stitches a minute could be knitted in this way by a skilled worker. Knitting sheaths were often made by young men for their sweethearts, carved with intertwined initials, hearts, flowers and even mottoes.

By the mid sixteenth century, knitting had become accepted as an important method of making fabric. A law of 1565 ruled that every person older than seven years had to wear, on pain of a fine, 'upon the Sabbath or holyday upon their head a cap of wool knitted, thickened and dressed in England'. Many of these knitted and felted woollen caps still exist in museums throughout the country. The caps were knitted, then the fabric was thickened by immersion in water for several days so the wool fibres felted together to make a solid mat. The cap was shaped and dried on a wooden block, then the surface was brushed with a teasel brush. This process resulted in a thick, warm fabric which could even be cut without the yarn unravelling. Today, the traditional French beret and Turkish fez are still made in the same way.

Towards the close of the sixteenth century, demand for knitted garments, particularly stockings for both men and women, began to outstrip production. William Lee, a graduate from Cambridge University, invented a rudimentary knitting machine between 1589 and 1600. Lee was unsuccessful in promoting his machine, which made stockings on a frame, mainly because its use was seen as a potential threat to the livelihood of handknitters. Gradually, however, the use of frames was developed. Although the Framework Knitters' Guild was granted a charter of incorporation as early as July 1657 and the days of commercial knitting by hand were in reality numbered, the development of mechanised knitting was very slow and hand knitting continued to flourish as a cottage industry for another 200 years.

Many knitted pieces survive from the seventeenth century, usually in the form of ecclesiastical vestments or ornate garments made for court wear for the aristocracy, and these include beautifully patterned altar gloves knitted in red silks and gold threads and the Italian silk undershirt worn by King Charles I at his execution in 1649.

KNITTING FOR LEISURE

As hand knitting gradually declined commercially, so the craft went through a revival as a purely domestic occupation. By the nineteenth century, the growth of a leisured class of women meant that much more time could be spent on working fine needlecrafts, particularly knitting, crochet and embroidery.

Intricate lace knitting worked in fine yarn on very fine needles became popular and many new lace stitches and patterns were invented during this period and used to make mittens, bonnets, shawls, tablecloths and layettes. Tiny glass and cut steel beads were threaded on to fine cotton or linen yarn and worked into intricately patterned purses and pincushions. Ladies' journals and magazines published knitting stitches and patterns regularly, but in the more remote communities it was still the tradition to pass on patterns by word of mouth from generation to generation.

The traditional colourwork patterns worked by knitters from the Fair Isles, for example, are reputed to have originated from Spanish sailors swept ashore after the ill-fated expedition of the Spanish Armada in 1588 when many of the defeated ships were wrecked by storms. The majority of Fair Isle patterns have survived unchanged throughout the centuries and are still worked from memory rather than from written instructions. Patterns for Shetland shawls, beautiful lacy creations so fine that some can be passed through a wedding ring without harm, are handed down in the same way.

Knitting has remained one of the most popular pastimes during this century, probably reaching a peak in the 1930s and 40s when the hand-knitted 'woollie' was in fashion.

Machine-made steel, and later aluminium and plastic, needles were inexpensive and readily available together with machine-spun and chemically dyed yarns. Magazines continued to publish a wide range of stitches and patterns, and there have been many excellent books published on the subject including Mary Thomas's books on stitches (*Book of Knitting Patterns*, 1943) and techniques (*Knitting Book*, 1938) and, more recently, Montse Stanley's *Handknitters' Handbook* (1986).

The more elaborate knitted lace pieces in this book, including the raised leaf Victorian bedspread (page 136) and the circular tablecloth (page 125), are from my collection of antique linen dating from the 1880s to the 1920s. My maternal grandmother, an expert knitter, used a raised leaf design similar to the bedspread motif when she knitted a colourful blanket for me during the early 1960s from her yarn oddments. I still treasure the blanket nearly thirty years later and, in spite of the occasional repair to a seam, the knitting is still going strong.

Specific yarns, hook sizes and tension have not been quoted for these designs, but the patterns have been written and charted for you to recreate these fine pieces of knitting and make heirlooms for your own family. A needle size/yarn thickness chart is given below to help you select the appropriate materials.

The remaining projects have been designed specially for this book, particularly with beginners in mind. The crystal bath salts jar on page 116 makes the ideal introduction to knitted lace, while the edging round the scented sachets (page 110) give the beginner useful practice at working an edging with points. Each project is graded with a degree-of-difficulty symbol so you can tell at a glance which projects are suitable for your level of experience and ability.

The pattern library on pages 142 to 155 contains over 30 more stitch patterns for knitted lace including eyelet and large-scale lace patterns for shawls and wraps, a border, motif and insertion featuring raised leaf designs, plus a selection of edgings, borders and insertions for decorating all items of household linen in various sizes, from towels to pillowcases.

NOTE FOR LEFT-HANDED READERS

When following the diagrams for working knitting stitches and techniques, prop the book up in front of a large mirror so the diagrams are reflected in reverse (ie left-handed) form.

NOTES FOR NORTH AMERICAN READERS

Both metric and imperial measurements are used throughout the book and there is a needle conversion chart on page 90. However, there are a few differences in knitting terminology and yarn names which are given below:

UK terms	US terms
Cast off	Bind off
Stocking stitch	Stockinette
Work straight	Work even
Tension	Gauge

UK yarn names	US yarn names
3 ply	Lightweight
4 ply	Fingering or mediumweight
Double knitting	Sport
Aran weight	Worsted or fisherman
Double-double or chunky	Heavyweight or bulky

Chart for knitted lace yarn weight/needle size combinations

Fine crochet cottons	1¼ mm–2¾ mm
2 ply	2¼ mm–3 mm
3 ply	2¾ mm–3¾ mm
4 ply	3 mm–4 mm
Double knitting	3¾ mm–4½ mm
Aran	4½ mm–5½ mm
Chunky	5½ mm–7½ mm

Practical Skills

There is a wide variety of yarns available which can be used to make knitted lace. Traditionally, this was worked in very fine cotton, linen or wool yarns but today almost any type of yarn with a smooth surface is acceptable. The weight of yarns you can use for working knitted lace varies from the finest mercerized cotton to double knitting weight wool. However, hairy yarns such as mohair and textured, knobbly yarns are not successful; a lace stitch pattern worked in mohair will be indistinct while a pattern worked in textured yarn will pull out of shape.

Yarn for knitting is usually sold ready-wound into balls of a specific size and the amount contained in each ball is quoted by weight rather than by length. The weight is given in grams or ounces – the most common ball sizes are 25 g or 50 g (1 oz or 2 oz) – and the length of yarn in the ball will vary from yarn to yarn depending on thickness. Occasionally, yarn is sold in coiled hanks or skeins and this must be wound by hand into balls before you start knitting. Fine cotton yarn is sold in a small, flattened ball wound round card or plastic and this type of yarn is usually labelled with length as well as weight.

Pure wool and wool/synthetic mixtures are formed by twisting together a number of strands or 'plies'. The finished yarns are available in several weights, from fine 2 ply to heavy, double-double knitting weight (also known as chunky). You can obtain a very fine Shetland wool, 1ply, spun specially for knitting traditional lacy Shetland shawls, but this is usually available only by mail order from spinners based in the Shetland Isles. Use the quoted ply as a general guide to the thickness of the yarn, as yarn measurements are not standard from spinner to spinner and the thickness will vary according to the degree of twist.

Thick cotton yarns are also available in 2-plies, 4-ply and double knitting. Many of the finer cotton yarns available in the shops are labelled as crochet cotton, and are particularly good for working knitted lace as these yarns are mercerized, making them smooth and very strong with a slightly glossy surface. The thickness of crochet yarns is graded by a series of numbers, from the coarsest (No 3) to the finest (No 60). In some countries very fine thread indeed, up to No 100, is available.

For the beginner, double-knitting weight wool or a wool/synthetic mixture is ideal for practising stitches, patterns and techniques. Wool retains a certain amount of

stretch and 'give' when it is spun into a yarn and this makes stitches easier to work. Begin by using a 4 mm knitting needles. When you have become familiar with using the wool yarn, change to a smooth cotton yarn of about the same thickness and work your stitches in this, again using a 4 mm needles. Cotton yarn is harder on the fingers than wool and has very little 'give' in it, but lace stitch patterns show up well. When you feel confident handling this weight of yarn and size of needles, move on to finer yarns and needles. The chart on page 87 gives information about needle sizes and suggests yarn weight/needle size combinations.

BALL BAND INFORMATION

Each ball of knitting yarn is wrapped in a paper band (called a ball band) which gives you lots of useful information about the yarn. As well as fibre composition and the weight of the ball, it will also show the colour and dye lot number, symbols for washing and pressing instructions and often a range of suitable needle sizes plus tension details. International yarn care symbols are shown below.

The dye lot number on the ball band is particularly important as when the yarn is dyed in batches there are often subtle variations in colour between lots. Although this difference may not be apparent when you compare balls of yarn in your hand, it will probably show as a shade variation when the yarn is knitted and may look unsightly. Always use yarn from the same dye lot for a single project.

Make sure you keep a ball band for each piece of knitted lace you work. Keep it in a small, polythene 'grip-top' bag with any left-over yarn and label the bag with details of the item you have made. You will then be able to refer to the washing instructions and have the correct yarn ready to make any necessary repairs.

NEEDLES AND OTHER EQUIPMENT

Knitting needles
Modern knitting needles are made from coated aluminium, plastic, bamboo or wood and all of them are light and easy to work with. Choice is really a matter of preference – some knitters prefer aluminium needles as they bend less easily than other types, while others choose plastic or bamboo as they are silent in use

Type of care	Dry cleaning	Washing	Bleaching	Drying	Ironing
Fairly easy care	(A) Use any dry-cleaning fluid	Machine-wash at stated temperature	Chlorine (household) bleach may be used	Can be tumble dried	High setting – hot
Treat carefully	(P) Use perchlorethylene or white spirit only	Hand wash at stated temperature		Dry on a line	Medium setting – warm
Handle with great care	(F) Use white spirit only	Wash by hand only		Allow to drip dry	Low setting – cool
Do not use treatment shown	Must not be dry-cleaned	Must not be washed	Do not use household bleach	Do not hang – lay flat	Must not be ironed

4 Slip the original stitch off the left-hand needle, leaving the new stitch on the right-hand needle. Repeat along the row until all the stitches have been transferred to the right-hand needle.

Purl stitch (p)

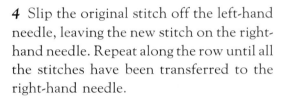

3 Pull a loop of yarn through to make a new stitch on the right-hand needle.
4 Slip the original stitch off the left-hand needle, leaving the new stitch on the right-hand needle. Repeat along the row until all the stitches have been transferred to the right-hand needle.

Knit two stitches together (k2 tog)

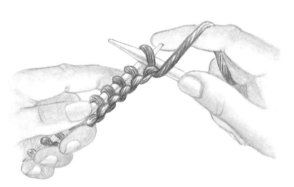

1 With the yarn at the front of the work, insert the right-hand needle through the front of the first in the row of stitches on the left-hand needle.

2 Wind the yarn round the right-hand needle as shown.

Decrease a stitch by inserting the right-hand needle through the front of the next two stitches on the left-hand needle and knit both stitches together. Work k3 tog in the same way, but knit three stitches instead of two.

Knit two stitches together through the back of the loop (k2 tog tbl)

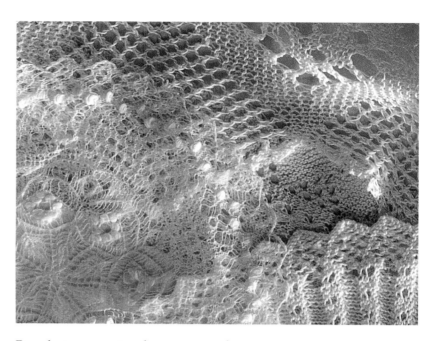

Work the same as k2 tog, but insert the right-hand needle through the back instead of the front of the two stitches.

Purl two stitches together (p2 tog)

Purl two stitches together through the back of the loop (p2 tog tbl)

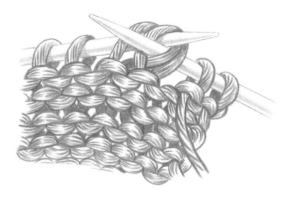

Decrease a stitch by inserting the right-hand needle through the front of the next two stitches on the left-hand needle and purl both stitches together. Work p3 tog in the same way, but purl three stitches instead of two.

Work the same as p2 tog, but insert the right-hand needle through the back instead of the front of the two stitches.

Slip one, knit one, pass slipped stitch over (sl 1, k1, psso)

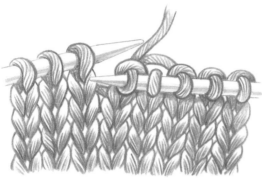

1 Slip the next stitch from the left-hand needle on to the right-hand needle without working it. Knit the next stitch on the left-hand needle in the usual way.

2 Using the left-hand needle point, lift the slipped stitch over the last stitch you have worked and off the right-hand needle to decrease one stitch.

Yarn over (yo)

In knitted lace, holes in the fabric are made by taking the yarn over the needle to make a loop which is worked as a stitch on the following row creating a hole. The yarn movement (the way in which the yarn is taken over the needle) depends on the stitches at either side, whether they are two knit stitches, two purl stitches, a knit and a purl stitch or a purl and a knit stitch. In this book, the abbreviation 'yo' is used for all these yarn movements unless otherwise stated.

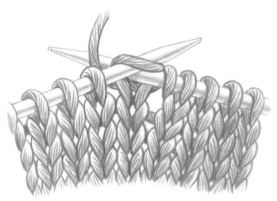

Working yo between two knit stitches
Bring the yarn forward to the front of the work between the needles and knit the next stitch in the usual way. The yarn makes an extra loop over the right-hand needle as you do this. Treat this loop as a stitch on the following row.

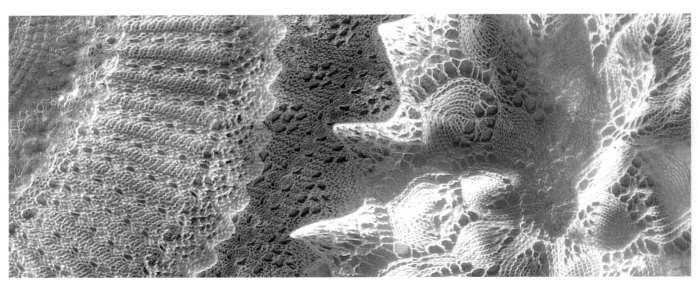

Working yo between two purl stitches
Take the yarn right round the right-hand needle point and bring it out at the front of the work ready to purl the next stitch. Treat the resulting loop as a stitch on the following row.

Working yo between a knit and a purl stitch Bring the yarn forward to the front of the work between the needles. Take the yarn over the right-hand needle and back to the front ready to purl the next stitch. Treat the resulting loop as a stitch on the following row.

Working yo between a purl and a knit stitch After working the purl stitch, the yarn is already at the front of the work. Proceed to knit the next stitch in the usual way. The yarn makes an extra loop over the right-hand needle as you do this. Treat this loop as a stitch on the following row.

Increase (inc)

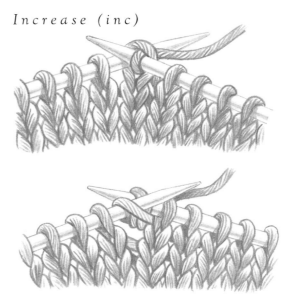

This can be worked in two ways:
1 Knit the next stitch on the left-hand needle in the usual way, but do not slip the original stitch from the left-hand needle. Knit again into this stitch, inserting the right-hand needle into the back of the stitch, then slip it off the needle. This makes two stitches from the original one.

2 Knit the next stitch on the left-hand needle in the usual way, but do not slip the original stitch from the left-hand needle. Instead, purl into this stitch before slipping it off the needle, making two new stitches from the original one.

Wherever the abbreviation 'inc' appears in this book, look under the special abbreviations section to find which method to use. Make sure you follow the correct instruction for the particular pattern you are using as the effect produced by these two methods looks different.

CASTING OFF

To make a soft, elastic cast-off edge, cast off in the same stitch you are using (ie either knit or purl) and use one or two sizes larger for the right-hand needle.

1 Knit the first two stitches in the usual way so they are both taken over on to the right-hand needle.

2 Using the left-hand needle point, lift the first stitch over the second stitch and off the needle.

3 Knit the next stitch so there are two stitches again on the right-hand needle and repeat step 2. Continue repeating steps 2 and 3 until there is one stitch remaining on the right-hand needle. Break off the yarn, lengthen the last stitch and pull the cut end through. Pull the yarn to tighten the stitch.

JOINING A NEW BALL OF YARN

Never, join a new ball of yarn in the middle of a row. This will not only look unsightly, but it makes a weak place in the knitting which may unravel in use. Instead, always make sure to join in the new yarn at the end of the row.

1 Knot the new yarn to the first stitch, leaving a long end to fasten off later.

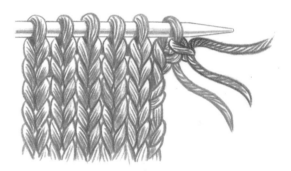

2 Work the first stitch with two yarns – one from the new ball and the end of the old yarn. Drop the old yarn and continue working with the new ball.

DOUBLE-POINTED NEEDLES

Knitting in the round on double-pointed needles can produce lovely circular pieces of knitted lace. When knitting with four needles, three needles hold the stitches in a triangular shape while the fourth (the working needle) is held in the right hand and used to knit the stitches. (The simplest way of thinking about the arrangement is to remember that the three needles holding the stitches represent the left-hand needle in conventional knitting and the fourth or working needle represents the right-hand needle.) When all the stitches from one needle have been worked, then that needle becomes the working needle.

Most circular knitting patterns use four needles, but some may use five or six. In this case, use one needle as the working needle and divide the stitches evenly between the remaining needles.

Although circular knitting may feel very cumbersome at first, it will become easier with practice. As the work is not turned at the end of each row in circular knitting, the right side of the knitting is always facing you. Take care to mark the beginning of each round with a marker.

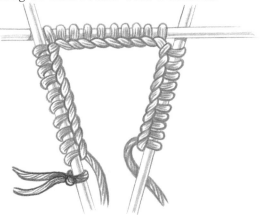

1 Cast the number of stitches stated in the pattern on to one of the needles. Divide the stitches equally between three needles and tie a loop of contrasting yarn on to the needle and the left-hand end of the

stitches. This loop marks the beginning of new rounds.

2 Arrange the needles in a triangle, taking care not to twist the stitches. Take the fourth needle and slip the marker loop on to it, then insert the needle into the first stitch on the third needle and knit the stitch. Continue knitting until all the stitches have been transferred to the fourth needle and the third needle then becomes the working needle.

Use the working needle to knit the stitches on the second needle then, in turn, use the new working needle to knit the stitches on the first needle to complete the first round. Pull the yarn tightly when changing needles to avoid holes forming and remember to transfer the marker loop at the beginning of every round.

KNITTING ABBREVIATIONS			
k	knit	*alt*	alternate
p	purl	*beg*	beginning
st(s)	stitch(es)	*foll*	following
k2 tog	knit two stitches together	*patt*	pattern
p2 tog	purl two stitches together	*tog*	together
tbl	through the back of loop(s)	*RS*	right side
sl	slip	*WS*	wrong side
psso	pass slipped stitch over	* repeat a sequence of stitches from that point	
yo	yarn over needle	[] the sequence inside square brackets must be repeated the given number of times	
rep	repeat		
rem	remaining	() round brackets contain extra information to help you, not instructions	
cont	continue		

HOW TO FOLLOW A WRITTEN PATTERN

Knitting patterns are written in a logical way, even though at first sight the instructions can look rather complicated. The most important thing to remember when following a pattern is to check that you cast on the correct number of stitches and then work through the instructions step by step *exactly* as stated.

Begin by reading the pattern through before you start to knit. As well as instructions, the pattern will contain information about materials, measurements and finishing off the item. Although some instructions or details may not be clear on the first reading, the technique involved will be much easier to grasp once the work is in front of you.

Many knitting abbreviations are standard and found in most patterns. A list of standard abbreviations and their meanings is given on page 99. Any special abbreviations are explained on the relevant pattern.

Asterisks

In order to make written patterns shorter and avoid tedious repetition, asterisks like this * are used to indicate which sections of the instructions have to be repeated across a row.

For example, an instruction such as 'K2, * k1, p4; rep from * to end' means that you begin the row by knitting the first two stitches, then you must work repeats of knit one stitch, purl four stitches right across the row until all the stitches on the left-hand needle have been used up.

Instead of the instruction 'rep from * to end', you may find something like 'rep from * to last 2 sts, k2'. In this case, work complete repeats of the instructions after the asterisk until there are only two stitches remaining on the needle, then you must knit these two stitches.

Square brackets

Square brackets [] fulfil a similar function to asterisks and both may be used in the same pattern row. Always repeat the sequence of stitches shown inside the square brackets for the stated number of times before proceeding to the next instruction in the row. For example, a pattern row reading 'K2, * K2, p4, [sl 1, k1, psso, k2 tog] twice, p4; rep from * to end' instructs you to knit the first two stitches, then work repeats of knit two, purl four, slip one, knit one, pass slipped stitch over, knit two together, slip one, knot one, pass slipped stitch over, knit two together, purl four, until all the stitches on the left-hand needle have been used up.

Round brackets

Round brackets () do not contain working instructions. Instead, they give extra information which the knitter may find helpful, for example the number of stitches which should be on the needle at the end of a particular row.

Repeats

Each stitch pattern is written using a specific number of pattern rows and row sequence must be repeated until the knitting is the correct length. A simple pattern such as the edging for the handkerchief on page 115 is four rows long, for example, while the deep edging on the towel on page 134 requires 32 rows of knitting to work one complete pattern repeat. In some of the more complex projects such as the fir trees tablecloth on page 118, specific sections of the pattern are repeated.

Where this is the case, the project instructions will tell you exactly which rows are to be repeated and which are to be worked once only.

When working a complicated stitch pattern, always make a note of exactly which row you are working. Use a row counter or write the row number in a notebook with a pencil as it's very easy to forget where you are when your knitting session gets interrupted by the doorbell or a telephone call. Avoid the temptation to use a pen when making notes as ink is rather messy and can be very difficult to remove from light-coloured yarn.

HOW TO FOLLOW A CHARTED PATTERN

Many knitters prefer working from a chart rather than from written instructions. Although a charted pattern still contains some written instructions, the most complicated part – the stitch pattern – is expressed in visual form. Traditionally, British patterns have been written rather than charted, but today there is a strong movement towards the charted stitch pattern which is used almost exclusively in other European countries. Charts also solve the problem of translating a long, complicated stitch pattern from one language to another.

To use a knitting chart, first familiarize yourself with the symbols and their meanings. These are given in the form of a key at the side of the chart. Each symbol represents a single instruction such as knit or purl, or a set of instructions such as knit two stitches together through the back of the loop. On some of the more complicated charts, such as the one for the pillowcase edging on page 112, some chart squares do not contain a symbol. These blank squares are used simply to make the chart a better shape and easier to follow.

Read knitting charts from the bottom, beginning at the right-hand edge of row 1 and working the first row from right to left across the chart. Work all the instructions on this row, then work row 2 from left to right in the same way. Read all the subsequent odd-numbered rows from right to left and even-numbered rows from left to

right. As a general rule, odd-numbered rows are right-side rows (the right side of the knitting is the one facing you as you work the row) and even-numbered rows are wrong-side rows (the back of the knitting is the one facing).

As when using written instructions, keep a note of which row you are working using a row counter or pad and pencil.

Knitting symbols

The chart shows the main symbols used in knitting charts. A key is also given beside each project and pattern library chart.

USING THE PATTERN LIBRARY

The pattern library pages give both written and charted instructions for a wide variety of stitch patterns. Many of these patterns can be substituted for project designs, particularly the edging and border patterns. A triangular raised leaf motif is given on page 154 which would make a lovely bedspread – work four motifs to make up each square and join the squares together in the same way as the Victorian bedspread on page 136. The large-scale lace patterns on page 146 can be substituted in the evening wrap on page 108.

To use the pattern library instructions, begin by casting on the correct number of stitches. For an edging, border or insertion, this number is given at the top of each pattern. Other patterns give you the correct number of stitches needed to work one complete pattern repeat. For example, the first line of the knotted trellis pattern on page 148 tells you to 'cast on a multiple of 6 sts plus 1'. This means that the total number of stitches to cast on so the pattern will be correct when knitted must be divisible by 6, and you must also add one extra stitch. So you could cast on say 61 stitches (6 × 10 + 1) or 73 (6 × 12 + 1) and the pattern would be correct in either case.

k1	k1
p1	p1
sl	sl
yo	yo
yo twice	yo twice
k1 tbl	k1 tbl
k2 tog	k2 tog
k2 tog tbl	k2 tog tbl
k3 tog	k3 tog
p2 tog	p2 tog
p2 tog tbl	p2 tog tbl
p3 tog	p3 tog
sl1, k1, psso	sl1, k1, psso
sl1, k2 tog, psso	sl1, k2 tog, psso
inc	inc
cast off 1st	cast off 1st
cast on 1st	cast on 1st
no stitch	no stitch

FINISHING TECHNIQUES

FINISHING OFF THREAD ENDS

Thread the end of the yarn through a tapestry needle and weave the point of the needle through several stitches on the wrong side of the knitting for at least 2.5 cm (1 in). Pull the needle and yarn through and cut off the yarn end.

PINNING OUT AND BLOCKING

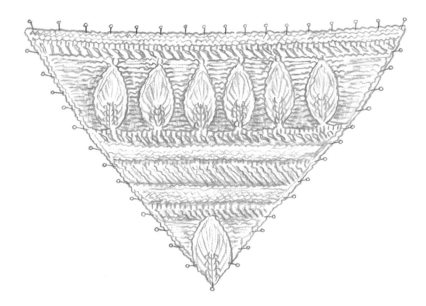

This process is essential for bringing out the delicate patterns in knitted lace and it can be used safely with either cotton, wool or wool/synthetic mixtures as no heat is applied. Although blocking may seem rather a lengthy process – a long strip may need pinning out in several sections and each section may take one or two days to dry out – the time will be well spent.

To pin out and block knitted lace you will need a large piece of blockboard or chipboard covered with thick cork floor tiles, brown paper, drawing pins, a sheet of polythene, stainless steel pins with glass or plastic heads and a small plant sprayer filled with cold water.

Using a pencil, draw the outline of the piece on to brown paper – for a border draw two parallel lines; for a circular piece, draw radiating lines from the centre corresponding with the number of motifs in the pattern; and for a square motif draw the correct size of square. Pin the brown paper on to the board with drawing pins and cover it with the polythene sheet.

Spray the knitting lightly with water and pin it out over the drawn shape using stainless steel pins. Adjust the pins until the knitting is stretched evenly, then spray with water once again, this time more heavily. Allow the knitting to dry completely at room temperature before removing the pins; the knitted fabric will retain the shape in which it dried. When blocking a border or edging, you will need to work in several sections, letting each portion of the work dry before moving on to the next section.

JOINING MOTIFS

After pinning and blocking all the knitted motifs to the same size, join them together by oversewing (see diagram) using the same yarn. Oversewing makes a very flat seam once it is opened out and pressed, unlike alternative methods which create an unsightly ridge.

Place two motifs together with right sides facing and the two edges to be joined aligning. Oversew along the edge, securing the thread carefully at the beginning and end of the stitching. Repeat this with further motifs until you have a strip of joined motifs which is the required length. Open out the seams and press them lightly on the wrong side. Make as many strips as you require, then join them together with oversewing, taking care to match up the short seams neatly.

APPLYING BORDERS, EDGING AND INSERTIONS

A border to a knitted bedspread

Place the knitted border on top of the bedspread with right sides facing and straight edges aligning. Pin in place, distributing the length of the border evenly along the sides and gathering it slightly at each corner so that the border will lie flat without pulling. Use long pins with glass or plastic heads so the pinheads will not pull through the knitting. Using a tapestry needle and the same yarn that you used for the knitting, oversew the layers together.

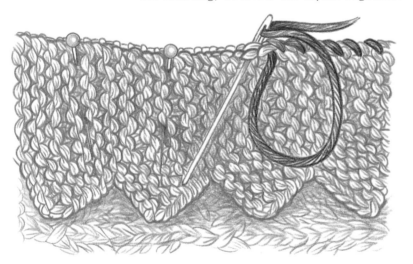

If you have used a very heavy yarn for the knitting, you will get a neater seam if you use a thinner thread, but don't be tempted to use sewing cotton as this will not be strong enough.

Attaching knitted lace edgings and borders to fabric

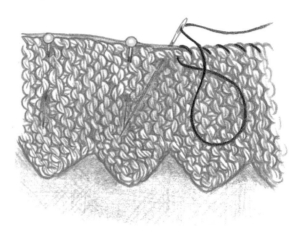

Position the edging or border on top of the hemmed edge of the fabric or towel with right sides facing and straight edges aligning. Make sure that the edging is evenly distributed and pin in place using glass-headed pins. Using a sewing needle and matching sewing cotton, stitch the knitting and fabric together using oversewing stitches. Make small, neat stitches and take care not to pull the thread too tightly. When attaching the edging to a corner, gather the knitting slightly so that the edging will lie flat when stitched in position.

Adding knitted lace insertions

Insertions are sewn between two pieces of fabric and are often used in conjunction with an edging or border. Pin the top of the insertion to the first piece of fabric with right sides facing and proceed as above. Then pin the lower edge of the insertion to the second piece of fabric and apply in the same way.

CARING FOR AND STORING KNITTED LACE

Follow the cleaning and pressing instructions on the ball band for the particular yarn you are using – a list of the international care symbols found on ball bands is given on page 89. If the yarn you have used is machine-washable, put the item into a clean white pillowcase to prevent it from being damaged and stretched during the machine cycle.

When not in use, store knitted lace wrapped in white, acid-free tissue paper in a cool and dry place. When folding a large item, pad the folds with tissue paper to prevent hard creases forming or, better still, roll it right-side out round a cardboard tube between layers of tissue paper.

When a little care, you can use and enjoy the knitted lace items you have made for years to come. Follow these simple guidelines:

○ Always wash knitted lace before it gets really soiled, taking prompt action to remove stains as soon as they occur, particularly on table-linen.

○ Repair holes and split seams as soon as you notice them to prevent further damage.

○ Keep items out of direct sunlight, especially during summer, as the sunlight will not only cause colours to fade, but it will eventually weaken the fibres.

Starching knitted lace

Articles trimmed with knitted lace edgings benefit from being starched after laundering. Choose a stiff-finish starch for small items such as placemats and table runners and a soft-finish one for tablecloths, napkins and other items which will be draped or folded in use.

The best method is to use soluble starch mixed with water (follow the manufacturer's instructions). Dip the article into the solution, squeeze out the moisture, then allow it to dry. Finish by pressing the piece with a hot iron.

Spray starch works well with small knitted items, but take care when ironing as spray starch may scorch when using a very hot iron.

Projects in knitted lace

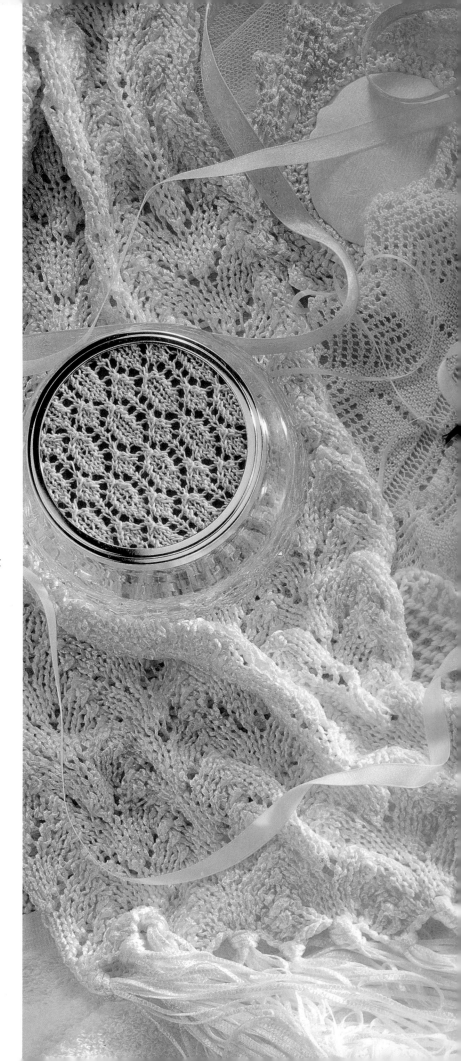

When selecting a project to make, choose one which reflects your present level of skill. Read right through the instructions before you begin to knit. You will also find it useful to work up one or more sample pieces to check the effect of your chosen yarn and hook. The following projects are aimed at people with varying levels of skill, from outright beginners to more experienced knitted lace enthusiasts. You'll find a symbol with one, two or three knitting needles at the start of each project. One needle indicates a very simple design, two indicates intermediate level and three needles are for more advanced projects which should only be attempted by a reader with considerable experience and patience.

EVENING WRAP

Soft, silky and glamorous, this evening wrap is knitted in a synthetic ribbon yarn, but you could substitute a pure wool yarn or a wool-and-mohair mixture, if you prefer. The eight-row pattern is not too difficult to knit and the work grows quickly on large needles. Four alternative patterns are given in the pattern library on page 149. Never press ribbon yarn, even with a cool iron, as the synthetic fibres will quickly become flattened and limp. Instead, pin out the knitting in sections, spray with cold water and allow them to dry naturally.

Materials
Cream double-knitting weight ribbon yarn
Pair of 4.5 mm knitting needles
Large crochet hook
Stretching board and pins
Scissors

Measurements
The wrap shown here measures approximately 33 cm (13 in) wide and was worked across 72 stitches. It measures 150 cm (59 in) long, excluding the fringe.

To make the wrap wider or narrower, simply add or subtract 10 stitches for each pattern repeat.

Working the wrap
To make a neat selvedge at each side of the wrap, slip the first stitch of each row knitwise before working the instructions to the end of the row, then knit the stitch remaining on the needle through the back of the loop.

Abbreviations
A full list of knitting abbreviations is given on page 99.

Cast on a multiple of 10 sts plus 2 for selvedges.
ROW 1 * yo, k3, sl 1, k2 tog, psso, k3, yo, k1; rep from * to end.
ROW 2 AND EVERY ALT ROW Purl.
ROW 3 * K1, yo, k2, sl 1, k2 tog, psso, k2, yo, k2; rep from * to end.
ROW 5 * K2, yo, k1, sl 1, k2 tog, psso, k1, yo, k3; rep from * to end.
ROW 7 * K3, yo, sl 1, k2 tog, psso, yo, k4; rep from * to end.
ROW 8 Purl.
Repeat rows 1 to 8 until the wrap reaches the required length, ending with an 8th row.
Cast off loosely knitwise.

Finishing the wrap
1 Sew in the ends. Pin out the knitting following the illustrated instructions given on page 102. Spray lightly with water and allow to dry thoroughly before removing the pins. Do not press. You will probably need to pin out the wrap in several sections to accommodate it on your board.
2 Cut 60 cm (24 in) lengths of yarn. Using the crochet hook, thread groups of six lengths of yarn at regular 2.5 cm (1 in) intervals along the short edges of the wrap. Knot the ends to form a fringe. Trim the ends of the fringe to an even length.

This luxurious and glamorous evening wrap can be worked in various yarns or wools. Here, it is knitted in ribbon yarn. Make a more elaborate fringe by knotting beads on to the strands.

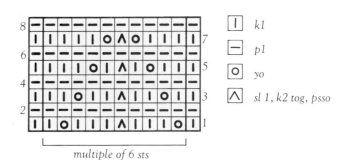

multiple of 6 sts

SCENTED SACHETS

Scented sachets make a delightful birthday or Christmas gift. These two sachets are made from white cotton fabric with a delicate woven pattern, but you could use scraps of printed cotton lawn and pick up the dominant print colour with the ribbon threaded through the edging. Here, a synthetic ribbon yarn is used to knit the edging, but almost any type of cotton or synthetic yarn could be substituted.
Fill the sachets with a little stuffing and a strongly scented pot pourri, such as dried rose petals.

Materials
Cream double knitting weight ribbon
  yarn
Scraps of self-patterned white cotton
  fabric
Pair of 3.5 mm knitting needles
Narrow white satin ribbon
Matching sewing thread
Sewing needle
Pins
Small amount of white polyester stuff-
  ing
Pot pourri

Measurements
Cut out two circles of fabric approximately 10 cm (4 in) in diameter for the sachet with the wide edging and two of the same size for the other sachet. The finished size of the sachet centres will be 8 cm (3 in) across and there is a seam allowance of 1 cm (½ in) all round. Knit the edging long enough to go round the circumference of the finished piece.

Abbreviations
A full list of knitting abbreviations is given on page 99.
Special abbreviation for this pattern:
inc = knit once onto the front and once into the back of the next stitch.

Working the wide edging
Cast on 8 sts and knit 1 row.
ROW 1 Sl 1, k2, [yo, k2 tog] twice, inc in last st.
ROWS 2, 4 AND 6 Knit.
ROW 3 Sl 1, k2, yo, k2 tog, k1, yo, k2 tog, inc in last st.
ROW 5 Sl 1, k2, yo, k2 tog, k2, yo, k2 tog, inc in last st.
ROW 7 Sl 1, k2, yo, k2 tog, k3, yo, k2 tog, inc in last st.
ROW 8 Cast off 4 sts, k7.
Repeat rows 1 to 8 until the edging is the required length, ending with an 8th row.
Cast off loosely knitwise.

Working the narrow edging
Cast on 5 sts and knit 1 row
ROW 1 Sl 1, k1, yo, k2 tog, inc in last st.
ROWS 2, 4 AND 6 Knit.
ROW 3 Sl 1, k2, yo, k2 tog, inc in last st.
ROW 5 Sl 1, k3, yo, k2 tog, inc in last st.
ROW 7 Sl 1, k4, yo, k2 tog, inc in last st.
ROW 8 Cast off 4 sts, k4.
Repeat rows 1 to 8 until the edging is the required length, ending with an 8th row.
Cast off loosely knitwise.

Making up the sachets
Both designs are made as follows:
1 Sew in the ends. Pin out the edging following the illustrated instructions given on page 102. Spray lightly with water and allow to dry completely before removing the pins. Do not press the ribbon yarn.
2 Pin two fabric circles together with right sides facing and machine stitch round the

Rich cream ribbon yarn edges these little sachets filled with scented pot pourri. They are very easy to knit and make an excellent beginner's project.

edge with a 1 cm (½ in) seam allowance, leaving a short opening for turning. Cut small notches into the raw edges, taking care not to cut into the stitching. Turn out through the opening and press lightly.

3 Fill the sachet with a mixture of polyester stuffing and pot pourri, then slipstitch the opening closed.

4 Pin the knitted edging evenly along the seam round the sachet and stitch in place using matching thread. Join the edges of the knitting in the same way. Thread the ribbon through a row of holes in the edging and tie into a neat bow.

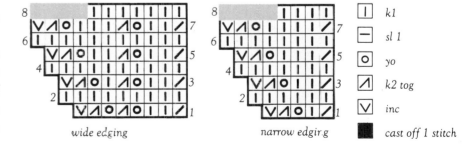

wide edging   *narrow edging*

I	k1
−	sl 1
o	yo
⼃	k2 tog
V	inc
■	cast off 1 stitch

WEDDING GIFT
BED LINEN

This unusual knitted edging decorates a pair of pristine white linen pillowcases to make a luxurious wedding gift for a special friend or relative. The edging is worked in fine cotton yarn and you can also make a longer matching strip to edge the top of a flat sheet.
Instructions and charts for four simpler knitted edgings are given on page 142 of the pattern library, and any of those could be substituted for the intricate design shown here. For knitters who find working with this weight of yarn a daunting and time-consuming task, why not knit two short strips of the edging pattern using double knitting weight cotton yarn and use them to trim a pair of white hand towels? When working your edging, choose a slightly larger needle size than usual as this pattern works best when the tension is fairly loose. You may need to knit several samples before finding the right combination.

Materials
White fine cotton yarn
Pair of white cotton or linen pillowcases
Pair of 3.25 mm knitting needles
Matching sewing thread
Sewing needle
Pins

Measurements
The original knitted edging measures approximately 6.5 cm (2½ in) across the widest point. For each pillowcase you will need to knit one strip of edging which is long enough to stretch right round the edge of the pillowcase and be gathered at each corner. To edge a flat sheet, work pattern repeats until your edging reaches the desired length.

Abbreviations
A full list of knitting abbreviations is given on page 99.
Special abbreviations for this pattern:
loop = cast on one stitch, then knit this stitch and the next stitch on the left-hand needle together wrapping the yarn twice round the needle
tog2 = knit the next two stitches on the left-hand needle together wrapping the yarn twice round the needle, then knit into the front of the first stitch again
inc1 = knit into the front and the back of the next stitch
yf = yarn forward to make a stitch
yrn2 = yarn round the needle twice
po = on left-hand needle, pass fourth, fifth and sixth stitches (in that order) over the first, second and third stitches and off the needle. When working yrn2 (yarn round the needle twice) it must be noted that on the following row this must have a k1 and p1 worked into the corresponding loops.

Working the edging
Cast on 26 sts.
ROW 1 (Right side facing) loop, k18, inc1, k6.
ROW 2 K4, p6, k17 dropping extra loop made on previous row.
ROW 3 Loop, k26.
ROW 4 Rep row 2.
ROW 5 Loop, k13, yf, k3, po, yrn2, k7.
ROW 6 K4, p3, k1, p1, k18 dropping extra loop made on previous row.
ROW 7 Loop, k19, inc1, k6.
ROW 8 K4, p6, k18 dropping extra loop made on previous row.

A treasured gift for the bridal couple, this exquisite bed linen is edged in a fine cotton yarn knitted at a fairly loose tension.

ROW 9 Loop, k12, yf, tog2, yf, k13.

ROW 10 K4, p6, k20 dropping extra loops made on previous row.

ROW 11 Loop, k12, turn.

ROW 12 K13 dropping extra loop made on previous row.

ROW 13 Loop, k11, k next 2 sts together but knitting into the front of both sts and then into the front of the first st again, k6, po, yrn 2, k7.

ROW 14 K4, p3, k1, p1, k20 dropping extra loop made on previous row.

ROW 15 Loop, k12, yf, [tog2, yf] twice, k5, inc1, k6.

ROW 16 K4, p6, k23 dropping extra loops made on previous row.

ROW 17 Loop, k32.

ROW 18 K4, p6, k23 dropping extra loop made on previous row.

ROW 19 Rep row 11.

ROW 20 Rep row 12.

ROW 21 Loop, k11, k next 2 sts together but knitting into the front of both sts and then into the front of the first st again, yf, [tog2, yf] 3 times, k3, po, yrn2, k7.

ROW 22 K4, p3, k1, p1, k16 dropping extra loops made on previous row, now working on sts on left-hand needle, pass 2nd, 3rd, 4th, 5th, 6th, 7th, 8th, 9th and 10th sts over first st, now k tog this first st with last st on needle dropping extra loop made on previous row. (26 sts)

Repeat these 22 rows for length of edging required, ending with a 22nd row.

Cast off loosely.

Attaching the edging

1 Pin out the edging in sections following the illustrated instructions given on page 102. Spray with water and allow to dry completely before removing the pins and moving on to the next section.

2 Pin the edging around the edge of the pillowcase, gently gathering the corners to fit and making sure you space out the edging evenly. Oversew the edging in place with matching sewing thread, taking care not to pull the stitches tight, then oversew the cast-on and cast-off edges together.

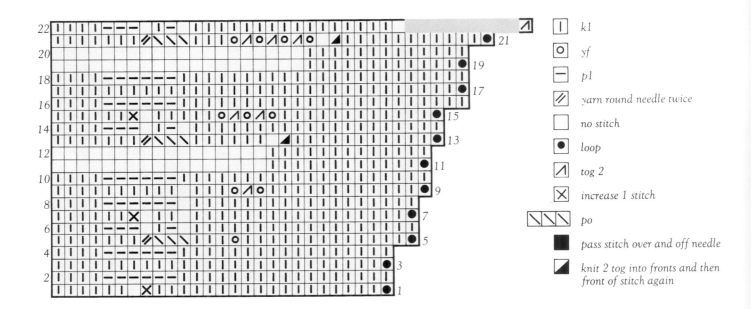

I	k1
o	yf
−	p1
⁄⁄	yarn round needle twice
□	no stitch
●	loop
⟋	tog 2
✕	increase 1 stitch
＼＼＼	po
▰	pass stitch over and off needle
◥	knit 2 tog into fronts and then front of stitch again

LACE-EDGED HANDKERCHIEF

Ready-made handkerchiefs are easily decorated with a narrow edging knitted in fine cotton yarn. Here, a beautifully embroidered handkerchief has been trimmed with a simple-to-knit, delicate edging. However, this edging would look equally effective on a plain white cotton or linen square.

When knitting the edging, remember to allow a little extra length so that it can be gathered at each corner; this will allow it to lie flat when stitched in place. The same edging can be used to decorate lingerie, nightwear and children's clothes.

Materials
White fine cotton yarn
White cotton or linen handkerchief
Pair of 2.5 mm knitting needles
Matching sewing thread
Sewing needle
Pins

Measurements
You will need to knit a strip of edging to go round the outside edge of the handkerchief, allowing a little extra so that the edging can be gathered slightly at each corner when it is stitched in place.

Abbreviations
Knitting abbreviations appear on page 99.

A delicate edging borders a beautiful cotton handkerchief. The pattern is easy to knit and can be used to edge a number of other small items.

Working the edging
Cast on 6 sts.
ROW 1 Sl 1, k1, yo, k2 tog, yo twice, k2.
ROW 2 Sl 1, k2, p1, k4.
ROW 3 Sl 1, k1, yo, k2 tog, k4.
ROW 4 [Sl 1, k1, psso] twice, k4.
Repeat rows 1 to 4 until the edging is
the required length, ending with a 4th
row.
Cast off loosely knitwise.

Attaching the edging
1 Sew in the ends. Pin out the edging
following the illustrated instructions given
on page 102. Spray lightly with water and
allow to dry completely before removing
the pins.
2 Beginning at the centre of one side, pin
the edging right round the edge of the
handkerchief, allowing a little extra at each
corner so the edging can be slightly gathered round the point.
3 Oversew the edging in place with matching sewing thread, taking care not to pull
the stitches tight. Join the short ends of the
knitting in the same way.

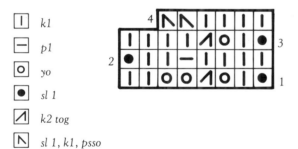

	k1
-	p1
o	yo
●	sl 1
∕	k2 tog
N	sl 1, k1, psso

CRYSTAL JAR COVER

A hand-cut crystal jar with silver-
edged glass lid provides the perfect
place for displaying a tiny piece of
delicate lace knitting. The pattern
shown here is perfectly suitable for a
beginner to work, especially as no
shaping is involved.
Starch your finished piece of
knitting stiffly before pinning it out
and allow it to dry thoroughly
before trimming and mounting it in
the lid surround. Here we have used
cream yarn backed with a pastel
paper, but you may prefer to choose
a brightly coloured yarn and show
off the knitting against a darker
background.

Materials
Cream fine cotton yarn
Crystal jar with self-assembly lid (see
  page 156)
Pair of 2.5 mm knitting needles
Stiff-finish starch
Scrap of coloured paper about 2.5 cm
  (1 in) larger than the jar lid
Scissors to cut knitting and paper

Measurements
You will need to knit a piece of lace
approximately 2.5 cm (1 in) larger all
round than your jar lid. Use the acetate
from the lid as a template around which to
cut the finished piece of knitting. Don't
worry if the piece turns out much larger
than the lid as any surplus can be cut away
quite easily after you have starched and
pinned out the lace.

Abbreviations

Knitting abbreviations appear on page 99.

Working the lace

Cast on a multiple of 6 sts plus 1. K1 row.

ROW 1 AND EVERY ALT ROW Purl.

ROWS 2, 4 AND 6 K1, * yo, sl 1, k1, psso, k1, k2 tog, yo, k1; rep from * to end.

ROW 8 K2, * yo, sl 1, k2 tog, psso, yo, k3; rep from *, ending last rep k2.

ROW 10 K1, * k2 tog, yo, k1, yo, sl 1, k1, psso, k1; rep from * to end.

ROW 12 K2 tog, * yo, k3, yo, sl 1, k2 tog, psso; rep from *, ending last rep yo, k3, yo, sl 1, k1, psso.

Repeat rows 1 to 12 until knitting is required length, ending with a 12th row. Cast off loosely knitwise.

Mounting the lace

1 Starch the lace stiffly. Pin out following the illustrated instructions on page 102 and allow to dry completely before removing the pins.

2 Centre the acetate from the jar lid on top of the stiffened lace and cut out the lace carefully, close to the edge. Cut out a piece of coloured paper in the same way.

3 Position the acetate inside the lid surround and cover it with the lace circle, placing it so the right side of the knitting is next to the acetate. Finally, add the coloured paper and backing piece. Carefully secure all the layers in the lid.

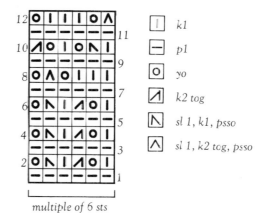

multiple of 6 sts

	k1
—	p1
O	yo
⟋	k2 tog
⟍	sl 1, k1, psso
⋀	sl 1, k2 tog, psso

FIR TREES TABLECLOTH

Make this pretty knitted border with its pattern of fir trees to edge a plain or lightly embroidered square tablecloth. The border appears deceptively simple but owing to its complex shaping and intricate edging it should only be attempted by the experienced knitter. As the border has shaped corners, you must knit the edging to the required size first, then cut your fabric to fit.

Materials
White fine mercerized cotton, No 40 or finer
White cotton or linen fabric
Pair of 2 mm knitting needles
White sewing thread
Sewing needle
Pins

Measurements
The border is made up of four identical pieces (see diagram). The original border measures 11 cm (4¼ in) at the widest point and each side contains 21 repeats of the centre 36-row portion of the chart.

Abbreviations
Knitting abbreviations appear on page 99.
Special abbreviations for this pattern:
yf = yarn forward
inc = knit into the front and then the back of the next stitch
yrn3 = yarn round needle three times. When working yrn3, the following row must have a k1, p1, k1 worked into the corresponding loops.

Working the border (make 4)
Cast on 4 sts.
ROW 1 *(RIGHT SIDE FACING)* Inc in first st, yrn3, k2 tog, inc in last st.
ROW 2 Inc in first st, k3, p1, k2, inc in last st.
ROW 3 Inc in first st, k6, k2 tog, k1.
ROW 4 K2 tog, using st on right-hand needle cast off 2 sts, k2, k2 tog, yf, k1, inc in last st.
ROW 5 Inc in first st, k4, yrn 3, k2 tog, inc in last st.
ROW 6 Inc in first st, k3, p1, k1, [k2 tog, yf] twice, k1, inc in last st.
ROW 7 Inc in first st, k10, k2 tog, k1.
ROW 8 K2 tog, using st on right-hand needle cast off 2 sts, k2, [k2 tog, yf] 3 times, k1, inc in last st.
ROW 9 Inc in first st, k8, yrn3, k2 tog, inc in last st.
ROW 10 Inc in first st, k3, p1, k1, [k2 tog, yf] 4 times, k1, inc in last st.
ROW 11 Inc in first st, k14, k2 tog, k1.
ROW 12 K2 tog, using st on right-hand needle cast off 2 sts, k2, [k2 tog, yf] 5 times, k2.
ROW 13 Inc in first st, k11, yrn3, k2 tog, inc in last st.
ROW 14 Inc in first st, k3, p1, k1, [k2 tog, yf] 6 times, k1.
ROW 15 Inc in first st, k16, k2 tog, k1.
ROW 16 K2 tog, using st on right-hand needle cast off 2 sts, k2, [k2 tog, yf] 6 times, k2.
ROW 17 Inc in first st, k13, yrn3, k2 tog, inc in last st.
ROW 18 Inc in first st, k3, p1, k1, [k2 tog, yf] 6 times, k3.
ROW 19 Inc in first st, k18, k2 tog, k1.
ROW 20 K2 tog, using st on right-hand needle cast off 2 sts, k2, [k2 tog, yf] 5 times, k6.
ROW 21 Inc in first st, k15, yrn3, k2 tog, inc in last st.
ROW 22 Inc in first st, k3, p1, k1, [k2 tog, yf] 4 times, k9.

This deep fir trees border is a challenge for the seasoned knitter, but the finished result is well worth the effort. The pattern is knitted in fine cotton.

ROW 23 Inc in first st, k20, k2 tog, k1.

ROW 24 K2 tog, using st on right-hand needle cast off 2 sts, k2, [k2 tog, yf] 3 times, k12.

ROW 25 Inc in first st, k17, yrn3, k2 tog, inc in last st.

ROW 26 Inc in first st, k3, p1, k1, [k2 tog, yf] twice, k15.

ROW 27 Inc in first st, k22, k2 tog, k1.

ROW 28 K2 tog, using st on right-hand needle cast off 2 sts, k2, k2 tog, yf, k18.

ROW 29 Inc in first st, k19, yrn3, k2 tog, inc in last st.

ROW 30 Inc in first st, k3, p1, k9, [k2 tog, yf] 6 times, k1.

ROW 31 Inc in first st, k24, k2 tog, k1.

ROW 32 K2 tog, using st on right-hand needle cast off 2 sts, k3, yf, k21.

ROW 33 Inc in first st, k18, k2 tog, k2, yrn3, k2 tog, inc in last st.

ROW 34 Inc in first st, k3, p1, k2, yf, k2 tog, yf, k20.

ROW 35 Inc in first st, k17, k2 tog, k8, k2 tog, k1.

ROW 36 K2 tog, using st on right-hand needle cast off 2 sts, k3, [yf, k2 tog] twice, yf, k19.

ROW 37 Inc in first st, yf, k2 tog, k14, k2 tog, k6, yrn3, k2 tog, inc in last st.

ROW 38 Inc in first st, k3, p1, k2, [yf, k2 tog] 3 times, yf, k18.

ROW 39 Inc in first st, k1, yf, [k2 tog, k12] twice, k2 tog, k1.

ROW 40 K2 tog, using st on right-hand needle cast off 2 sts, k3, [yf, k2 tog] 4 times, yf, k14, yf, k2 tog, k1.

ROW 41 Inc in first st, k2, yf, [k2 tog, k10] twice, yrn3, k2 tog, inc in last st.

ROW 42 Inc in first st, k3, p1, k2, [yf, k2 tog] 5 times, yf, k12, yf, k2 tog, k2.

ROW 43 Inc in first st, k3, yf, k2 tog, k8, k2 tog, k16, k2 tog, k1.

ROW 44 K2 tog, using st on right-hand needle cast off 2 sts, k3, [yf, k2 tog] 6 times, yf, k10, yf, k2 tog, k3.

ROW 45 Inc in first st, k4, yf, k2 tog, k6, k2 tog, k14, yrn3, k2 tog, inc in last st.

ROW 46 Inc in first st, k3, p1, k2, [yf, k2 tog] 7 times, yf, k8, yf, k2 tog, k4.

ROW 47 Inc in first st, k5, yf, k2 tog, k4, k2 tog, k20, k2 tog, k1.

ROW 48 K2 tog, using st on right-hand needle cast off 2 sts, k3, [yf, k2 tog] 8 times, yf, k6, yf, [k2 tog] twice, k3.

ROW 49 Inc in first st, k1, yrn3, k2 tog, k2, yf, [k2 tog] twice, k18, yrn3, k2 tog, inc in last st.

ROW 50 Inc in first st, k3, p1, k1, [k2 tog, yf] 8 times, k7, yf, k2 tog, k2, p1, k4.

ROW 51 Inc in first st, k8, yf, k2 tog, k25, k2 tog, k1.

ROW 52 K2 tog, using st on right-hand needle cast off 2 sts, k2, [k2 tog, yf] 7 times, k9, yf, [k2 tog] twice, k6.

ROW 53 Inc in first st, yf, [k2 tog] twice, yrn3, k2 tog, k2, yf, k2 tog, k21, yrn3, k2 tog, inc in last st.

ROW 54 Inc in first st, k3, p1, k1, [k2 tog, yf] 6 times, k11, yf, k2 tog, k2, p1, k4, yf, k2 tog.

ROW 55 Inc in first st, k1, yf, k2 tog, k7, yf, k2 tog, k25, k2 tog, k1.

ROW 56 K2 tog, using st on right-hand needle cast off 2 sts, k2, [k2 tog, yf] 5 times, k13, yf, [k2 tog] twice, k5, yf, k2 tog, k1.

The shaping of the first corner is now complete. Now begin the centre section:

ROW 57 Sl 1, k2, yf, [k2 tog] twice, yrn3, k2 tog, k2, yf, k2 tog, k21, yrn3, k2 tog, inc in last st.

ROW 58 Inc in first st, k3, p1, k1, [k2 tog, yf] 4 times, k15, yf, k2 tog, k2, p1, k4, yf, k2 tog, k1.

ROW 59 Sl 1, k2, yf, k2 tog, k7, yf, k2 tog, k25, k2 tog, k1.

ROW 60 K2 tog, using st on right-hand needle cast off 2 sts, k2, [k2 tog, yf] 3 times, k17, yf, [k2 tog] twice, k5, yf, k2 tog, k1.

ROW 61 Sl 1, k2, yf, [k2 tog] twice, yrn3,

k2 tog, k2, yf, k2 tog, k21, yrn3, k2 tog,
inc in last st.
ROW 62 Inc in first st, k3, p1, k1, [k2 tog,
yf] twice, k19, yf, k2 tog, k2, p1, k4, yf,
k2 tog, k1.
ROW 63 Sl 1, k2, yf, k2 tog, k7, yf, k2
tog, k25, k2 tog, k1.
ROW 64 K2 tog, using st on right-hand
needle cast off 2 sts, k2, k2 tog, yf, k21,
yf, [k2 tog] twice, k5, yf, k2 tog, k1.

Now work the following 36 rows which
form the pattern repeat:
ROW 1 (RIGHT SIDE FACING) Sl 1, k2, yf, [k2
tog] twice, yrn3, k2 tog, k2, yf, k2 tog,
k21, yrn3, k2 tog, inc in last st.
ROW 2 Inc in first st, k3, p1, k9, [k2 tog,
yf] 6 times, k3, yf, k2 tog, k2, p1, k4,
yf, k2 tog, k1.
ROW 3 Sl 1, k2, yf, k2 tog, k7, yf, k2 tog,
k25, k2 tog, k1.
ROW 4 K2 tog, using st on right-hand
needle cast off 2 sts, k3, yf, k22, yf, [k2
tog] twice, k5, yf, k2 tog, k1.
ROW 5 Sl 1, k2, yf, [k2 tog] twice, yrn3,
k2 tog, k2, yf, k2 tog, k18, k2 tog, k2,
yrn3, k2 tog, inc in last st.
ROW 6 Inc in first st, k3, p1, k2, yf, k2
tog, yf, k20, yf, k2 tog, k2, p1, k4, yf,
k2 tog, k1.
ROW 7 Sl 1, k2, yf, k2 tog, k7, yf, k2 tog,
k16, k2 tog, k8, k2 tog, k1.
ROW 8 K2 tog, using st on right-hand
needle cast off 2 sts, k3, yf, [k2 tog, yf]
twice, k18, yf, [k2 tog] twice, k5, yf, k2
tog, k1.
ROW 9 Sl 1, k2, yf, [k2 tog] twice, yrn3,
k2 tog, k2, yf, k2 tog, k14, k2 tog, k6,
yrn3, k2 tog, inc in last st.
ROW 10 Inc in first st, k3, p1, k2, yf, [k2
tog, yf] 3 times, k16, yf, k2 tog, k2, p1,
k4, yf, k2 tog, k1.
ROW 11 Sl 1, k2, yf, k2 tog, k7, yf, [k2
tog, k12] twice, k2 tog, k1.
ROW 12 K2 tog, using st on right-hand
needle cast off 2 sts, k3, yf, [k2 tog, yf]

4 times, k14, yf, [k2 tog] twice, k5, yf,
k2 tog, k1.
ROW 13 Sl 1, k2, yf, [k2 tog] twice, yrn3,
k2 tog, k2, yf, [k2 tog, k10] twice, yrn3,
k2 tog, inc in last st.
ROW 14 Inc in first st, k3, p1, k2, yf, [k2
tog, yf] 5 times, k12, yf, k2 tog, k2, p1,
k4, yf, k2 tog, k1.
ROW 15 Sl 1, k2, yf, k2 tog, k7, yf, k2
tog, k8, k2 tog, k16, k2 tog, k1.
ROW 16 K2 tog, using st on right-hand
needle cast off 2 sts, k3, yf, [k2 tog, yf]
6 times, k10, yf, [k2 tog] twice, k5, yf,
k2 tog, k1.
ROW 17 Sl 1, k2, yf, [k2 tog] twice, yrn3,
k2 tog, k2, yf, k2 tog, k6, k2 tog, k14,
yrn3, k2 tog, inc in last st.
ROW 18 Inc in first st, k3, p1, k2, yf, [k2
tog, yf] 7 times, k8, yf, k2 tog, k2, p1,
k4, yf, k2 tog, k1.
ROW 19 Sl 1, k2, yf, k2 tog, k7, yf, k2
tog, k4, k2 tog, k20, k2 tog, k1.
ROW 20 K2 tog, using st on right-hand
needle cast off 2 sts, k3, yf, [k2 tog, yf]
8 times, k6, yf, [k2 tog] twice, k5, yf, k2
tog, k1.
ROW 21 Sl 1, k2, yf, [k2 tog] twice, yrn3,
k2 tog, k2, yf, k2 tog, k2, k2 tog, k18,
yrn3, k2 tog, inc in last st.
ROW 22 Inc in first st, k3, p1, k1, [k2 tog,
yf] 8 times, k7, yf, k2 tog, k2, p1, k4,
yf, k2 tog, k1.
ROW 23 Sl 1, k2, yf, k2 tog, k7, yf, k2
tog, k25, k2 tog, k1.
ROW 24 K2 tog, using st on right-hand
needle cast off 2 sts, k2, [k2 tog, yf] 7
times, k9, yf, [k2 tog] twice, k5, yf, k2
tog, k1.
ROW 25 Sl 1, k2, yf, [k2 tog] twice, yrn3,
k2 tog, k2, yf, k2 tog, k21, yrn3, k2 tog,
inc in last st.
ROW 26 Inc in first st, k3, p1, k1, [k2 tog,
yf] 6 times, k11, yf, k2 tog, k2, p1, k4,
yf, k2 tog, k1.
ROW 27 Sl 1, k2, yf, k2 tog, k7, yf, k2
tog, k25, k2 tog, k1.

ROW 28 K2 tog, using st on right-hand needle cast off 2 sts, k2, [k2 tog, yf] 5 times, k13, yf, [k2 tog] twice, k5, yf, k2 tog, k1.

ROW 29 Sl 1, k2, yf, [k2 tog] twice, yrn3, k2 tog, k2, yf, k2 tog, k21, yrn3, k2 tog, inc in last st.

ROW 30 Inc in first st, k3, p1, k1, [k2 tog, yf] 4 times, k15, yf, k2 tog, k2, p1, k4, yf, k2 tog, k1.

ROW 31 Sl 1, k2, yf, k2 tog, k7, yf, k2 tog, k25, k2 tog, k1.

ROW 32 K2 tog, using st on right-hand needle cast off 2 sts, k2, [k2 tog, yf] 3 times, k17, yf, [k2 tog] twice, k5, yf, k2 tog, k1.

ROW 33 Sl 1, k2, yf, [k2 tog] twice, yrn3, k2 tog, k2, yf, k2 tog, k21, yrn3, k2 tog, inc in last st.

ROW 34 Inc in first st, k3, p1, k1, [k2 tog, yf] twice, k19, yf, k2 tog, k2, p1, k4, yf, k2 tog, k1.

ROW 35 Sl 1, k2, yf, k2 tog, k7, yf, k2 tog, k25, k2 tog, k1.

ROW 36 K2 tog, using st on right-hand needle cast off 2 sts, k2, k2 tog, yf, k21, yf, [k2 tog] twice, k5, yf, k2 tog, k1. Repeat last 36 rows 21 times, or as many times as necessary. Then work rows 1 to 10 again.

Now start the decrease of the border:

ROW 1 (RS FACING) K2 tog, k1, yf, k2 tog, k7, yf, [k2 tog, k12] twice, k2 tog, k1.

ROW 2 K2 tog, using st on right-hand needle cast off 2 sts, k3, yf, [k2 tog, yf] 4 times, k14, yf, [k2 tog] twice, k5, yf, k2 tog.

ROW 3 K2 tog, yf, [k2 tog] twice, yrn3, k2 tog, k2, yf, [k2 tog, k10] twice, yrn3, k2 tog, inc in last st.

ROW 4 Inc in first st, k3, p1, k2, yf, [k2 tog, yf] 5 times, k12, yf, k2 tog, k2, p1, k5.

	k1
O	yf
⟋	k2 tog
−	p1
●	slip 1 stitch
X	increase 1 stitch
⧄	yarn round needle 3 times
	no stitch
■	cast off stitch

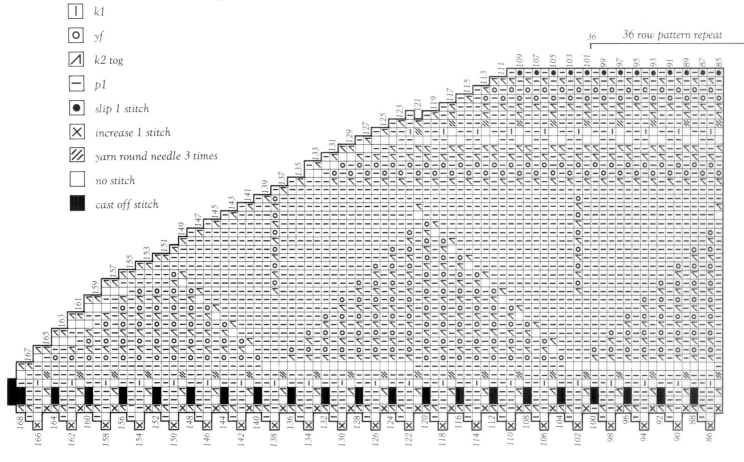

36 row pattern repeat

ROW 5 K2 tog, k8, yf, k2 tog, k8, k2 tog, k16, k2 tog, k1.

ROW 6 K2 tog, using st on right-hand needle cast off 2 sts, k3, yf, [k2 tog, yf] 6 times, k10, yf, [k2 tog] twice, k5.

ROW 7 [K2 tog] twice, yrn3, k2 tog, k2, yf, k2 tog, k6, k2 tog, k14, yrn3, k2 tog, inc in last st.

ROW 8 Inc in first st, k3, p1, k2, yf, [k2 tog, yf] 7 times, k8, yf, k2 tog, k2, p1, k3.

ROW 9 K2 tog, k6, yf, k2 tog, k4, k2 tog, k20, k2 tog, k1.

ROW 10 K2 tog, using st on right-hand needle cast off 2 sts, k3, yf, [k2 tog, yf] 8 times, k6, yf, [k2 tog] twice, k3.

ROW 11 K2 tog, yrn3, k2 tog, k2, yf, k2 tog, k2, k2 tog, k18, yrn3, k2 tog, inc in last st.

ROW 12 Inc in first st, k3, p1, k1, [k2 tog, yf] 8 times, k7, yf, k2 tog, k2, p1, k2.

ROW 13 K2 tog, k5, yf, k2 tog, k25, k2 tog, k1.

ROW 14 K2 tog, using st on right-hand needle cast off 2 sts, k2, [k2 tog, yf] 7 times, k9, yf, [k2 tog] twice, k2.

ROW 15 K2 tog, k3, yf, k2 tog, k21, yrn3, k2 tog, inc in last st.

ROW 16 Inc in first st, k3, p1, k1, [k2 tog, yf] 6 times, k11, yf, k2 tog, k2.

ROW 17 K2 tog, k2, yf, k2 tog, k25, k2 tog, k1.

ROW 18 K2 tog, using st on right-hand needle cast off 2 sts, k2, [k2 tog, yf] 5 times, k13, yf, k2 tog, k1.

ROW 19 K2 tog, k1, yf, k2 tog, k21, yrn3, k2 tog, inc in last st.

ROW 20 Inc in first st, k3, p1, k1, [k2 tog, yf] 4 times, k15, yf, k2 tog.

ROW 21 K2 tog, yf, k2 tog, k25, k2 tog, k1.

ROW 22 K2 tog, using st on right-hand needle cast off 2 sts, k2, [k2 tog, yf] 3 times, k18.

ROW 23 K2 tog, k22, yrn3, k2 tog, inc in last st.

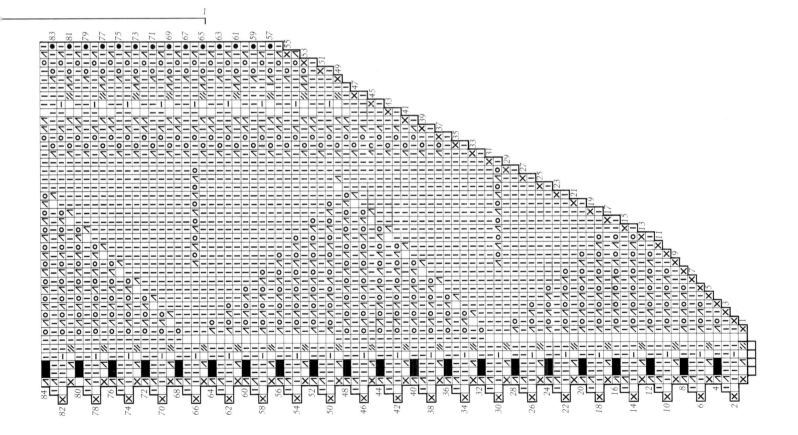

ROW 24 Inc in first st, k3, p1, k1, [k2 tog, yf] twice, k19.

ROW 25 K2 tog, k25, k2 tog, k1.

ROW 26 K2 tog, using st on right-hand needle cast off 2 sts, k2, k2 tog, yf, k20.

ROW 27 K2 tog, k20, yrn3, k2 tog, inc in last st.

ROW 28 Inc in first st, k3, p1, k9, [k2 tog, yf] 6 times, k1.

ROW 29 K2 tog, k23, k2 tog, k1.

ROW 30 K2 tog, using st on right-hand needle cast off 2 sts, k3, yf, k19.

ROW 31 K2 tog, k15, k2 tog, k2, yrn3, k2 tog, inc in last st.

ROW 32 Inc in first st, k3, p1, k2, yf, k2 tog, yf, k16.

ROW 33 K2 tog, k12, k2 tog, k8, k2 tog, k1.

ROW 34 K2 tog, using st on right-hand needle cast off 2 sts, k3, yf, [k2 tog, yf] twice, k13.

ROW 35 K2 tog, k9, k2 tog, k6, yrn3, k2 tog, inc in last st.

ROW 36 Inc in first st, k3, p1, k2, yf, [k2 tog, yf] 3 times, k10.

ROW 37 K2 tog, k6, k2 tog, k12, k2 tog, k1.

ROW 38 K2 tog, using st on right-hand needle cast off 2 sts, k3, yf, [k2 tog, yf] 4 times, k7.

ROW 39 K2 tog, k3, k2 tog, k10, yrn3, k2 tog, inc in last st.

ROW 40 Inc in first st, k3, p1, k2, yf, [k2 tog, yf] 5 times, k2, k2 tog.

ROW 41 K2 tog, k17, k2 tog, k1.

ROW 42 K2 tog, using st on right-hand needle cast off 2 sts, k3, yf, [k2 tog, yf] 4 times, k3, k2 tog.

ROW 43 K2 tog, k12, yrn3, k2 tog, inc in last st.

ROW 44 Inc in first st, k3, p1, k2, yf, [k2 tog, yf] 4 times, k2, k2 tog.

ROW 45 K2 tog, k15, k2 tog, k1.

ROW 46 K2 tog, using st on right-hand needle cast off 2 sts, k3, yf, [k2 tog, yf] 3 times, k2 tog, k1, k2 tog.

ROW 47 K2 tog, k9, yrn3, k2 tog, inc in last st.

ROW 48 Inc in first st, k3, p1, k2, yf, [k2 tog, yf] twice, k2 tog, k1, k2 tog.

ROW 49 K2 tog, k11, k2 tog, k1.

ROW 50 K2 tog, using st on right-hand needle cast off 2 sts, k3, [yf, k2 tog] twice, k1, k2 tog.

ROW 51 K2 tog, k5, yrn3, k2 tog, inc in last st.

ROW 52 Inc in first st, k3, p1, k2, yf, k2 tog, k1, k2 tog.

ROW 53 K2 tog, k7, k2 tog, k1.

ROW 54 K2 tog, using st on right-hand needle cast off 2 sts, k3, yf, k1, k2 tog.

ROW 55 K2 tog, k2, yrn3, k2 tog, inc in last st.

ROW 56 Inc in first st, k3, p1, k2, k2 tog.

ROW 57 K2 tog, k4, k2 tog, k1.

ROW 58 K2 tog, using st on right-hand needle cast off 2 sts, k1, k2 tog (3 sts). Cast off rem 3 sts.

Making up the tablecloth

1 Sew in the ends. Pin out the border a section at a time following the instructions given on page 102, taking special care with the corner sections. Spray with water and allow each section to dry before moving on to the next section.

2 Join the short ends of the border, matching the pattern carefully and using small, neat stitches and matching sewing thread. Pin the border roughly on to the fabric, making sure that the fir tree motifs are evenly spaced along each side. Carefully trim the fabric to fit, allowing a 3 cm (1¼ in) hem allowance all round. Remove the pins. Turn, pin and tack a double 1.5 cm (⅝ in) hem round the cloth. Hand or machine-stitch using matching thread.

3 Pin the border round the cloth, spacing the motifs evenly. Using small, neat stitches and matching sewing thread, oversew the border to the tablecloth. Finally, press lightly on the wrong side with a warm iron.

CIRCULAR TEA CLOTH

This delightful circular cloth features a lace petal and leaf design set off with a feather-and-fan border. It is knitted in rounds from the centre outwards. Begin by using a set of four double-pointed needles, then move on to a circular needle, changing lengths as required. Designed to be worked by an expert knitter who has had experience in knitting in the round, the lace cloth would look attractive laid over a plain cloth in a deep colour which would show off the intricacy of the design. Alternatively, it could be used alone as the centrepiece on a polished wooden dining table. When all the knitting has been completed, sew in the ends and spend some time pinning out and blocking the cloth to enhance the beauty of the wave-patterned edging.

Materials
Ecru fine cotton yarn
Set of four double-pointed knitting needles and a circular needle, changing lengths as required
Pins

Measurement
The original cloth measures 1 m (39½ in) in diameter.

Abbreviations
Knitting abbreviations appear on page 99. Special abbreviations for this pattern:
yf = yarn forward – note that this abbreviation is also used for yarn round needle
psso = pass slipped stitch over
skpo = sl 1, k1, psso
k1B = knit into back of stitch
inc = increase one stitch

Working the cloth
Using a set of four needles cast on 10 sts (3 sts on each of 2 needles and 4 sts on the 3rd needle).

Join into a circle and work in rounds.

Mark beginning of round with a coloured thread and move this marker as required.

ROUND 1 [Yf, k1] 10 times – 20 sts.
ROUND 2 AND EVERY ALTERNATE ROUND Knit.
ROUND 3 [K1, inc in next st] 10 times – 30 sts.
ROUND 5 [K1, yf, k1, yf, k1] 10 times – 50 sts.
ROUND 7 [K2, yf, k1, yf, k2] 10 times.
ROUND 9 [K3, yf, k1, yf, k3] 10 times.
ROUND 11 [K4, yf, k1, yf, k4] 10 times.
ROUND 13 [K5, yf, k1, yf, k5] 10 times.
ROUND 15 [Yf, k6, yf, k1, yf, k6] 10 times.
ROUND 17 [K1, yf, skpo, k11, k2 tog, yf] 10 times.
ROUND 19 [K1, yf, k1, skpo, k9, k2 tog, k1, yf] 10 times.
ROUND 21 [K1, yf, k2, skpo, k7, k2 tog, k2, yf] 10 times.
ROUND 23 [K1, yf, k3, skpo, k5, k2 tog, k3, yf] 10 times.
ROUND 25 [K1, yf, k4, skpo, k3, k2 tog, k4, yf] 10 times.
ROUND 27 [K1, yf, k5, skpo, k1, k2 tog, k5, yf] 10 times.
ROUND 29 [K1, yf, k6, sl 1, k2 tog, psso, k6, yf] 10 times – 160 sts.
ROUND 31 [K1, yf, k5, k2 tog, yf, k1, yf, skpo, k5, yf] 10 times.
ROUND 33 [K6, k2 tog, k1, yf, k1, yf, k1, skpo, k5] 10 times.
ROUND 35 [K5, k2 tog, k2, yf, k1, yf, k2, skpo, k4] 10 times.
ROUND 37 [K4, k2 tog, k3, yf, k1, yf, k3,

skpo, k3] 10 times.

ROUND 39 [K3, k2 tog, k4, yf, k1, yf, k4, skpo, k2] 10 times.

ROUND 41 [K2, k2 tog, k5, yf, k1, yf, k5, skpo, k1] 10 times.

ROUND 43 [K1, k2 tog, k6, yf, k1, yf, k6, skpo] 10 times.

ROUND 45 Sl last st of last round onto beg of new round then work as follows: [Sl 1, k2 tog, psso, yf, k7, yf, k1, yf, k7, yf] 10 times – 200 sts.

ROUND 47 [K2, yf, k8, yf, k1, yf, k8, yf, k1] 10 times.

ROUND 49 Sl last st of last round onto beg of new round then work as follows: [Sl 1, k2 tog, psso, yf, k1b, yf, skpo, k7, yf, k1, yf, k7, k2 tog, yf, k1B, yf] 10 times.

ROUND 51 [K1B, yf, k3, yf, skpo, k7, yf, k1, yf, k7, k2 tog, yf, k3, yf] 10 times.

ROUND 53 Sl last st of last round onto beg of new round then work as follows: [Sl 1, k2 tog, psso, yf, sl 1, k2 tog, psso, yf, k1B, yf, skpo, k15, k2 tog, yf, k1B, yf, sl 1, k2 tog, psso, yf] 10 times.

ROUND 55 [K3, yf, k1B, yf, k3, yf, skpo, k13, k2 tog, yf, k3, yf, k1B, yf] 10 times.

ROUND 57 [* Yf, sl 1, k2 tog, psso; rep from * 3 times in all, yf, k1B, yf, skpo, k11, k2 tog, yf, k1B, ** yf, sl 1, k2 tog, psso; rep from ** once more] 10 times.

ROUND 59 [K1, yf, k1B, yf, k3, yf, k1B, yf, k3, yf, skpo, k9, k2 tog, yf, k3, yf, k1B, yf, k2] 10 times.

ROUND 61 Sl first st of next round onto end of last round then work as follows: [* Yf, sl 1, k2 tog, psso; rep from * 4 times in all, yf, k1B, yf, skpo, k7, k2 tog, yf, k1B, ** yf, sl 1, k2 tog, psso; rep from ** 3 times in all] 10 times.

ROUND 63 [* K3, yf, k1B, yf; rep from * once more, k3, yf, skpo, k5, k2 tog, yf, ** k3, yf, k1B, yf; rep from ** once more] 10 times.

ROUND 65 [* Yf, sl 1, k2 tog, psso; rep from * 5 times in all, yf, k1B, yf, skpo, k3, k2 tog, yf, k1B, ** yf, sl 1, k2 tog, psso; rep from ** 4 times in all] 10 times.

ROUND 67 [K1, * yf, k1B, yf, k3; rep from * 3 times in all, yf, skpo, k1, k2 tog, ** yf, k3, yf, k1B; rep from ** once more, yf, k2] 10 times.

ROUND 69 Sl first st of next round onto end of last round then work as follows: [* Yf, sl 1, k2 tog, psso; rep from * 6 times in all, yf, k1B, yf, sl 1, k2 tog, psso, yf, k1B, ** yf, sl 1, k2 tog, psso; rep from ** 5 times in all] 10 times.

ROUND 71 [* K3, yf, k1B, yf; rep from * 7 times in all] 10 times.

ROUND 73 [* Yf, sl 1, k2 tog, psso; rep from * 14 times in all] 10 times.

ROUND 75 [* K1, yf, k1B, yf, K2; rep from * 7 times in all] 10 times.

ROUND 77 Sl first st of next round onto end of last round then work as follows: [* Yf, sl 1, k2 tog, psso; rep from * 14 times in all] 10 times.

ROUND 79 [* K3, yf, k1B, yf; rep from * 7 times in all] 10 times.

ROUND 81 [* Yf, sl 1, k2 tog, psso; rep from * 14 times in all] 10 times.

ROUND 83 [* K1, yf, k1B, yf, k2; rep from * 7 times in all] 10 times.

ROUND 85 Sl first st of next round onto end of last round then work as follows: [* Yf, sl 1, k2 tog, psso; rep from * 14 times in all] 10 times.

ROUND 87 [* K3, yf, k1B, yf; rep from * 7 times in all] 10 times.

Note: pattern is now repeated 5 times in the round.

ROUND 89 [* (Yf, sl 1, k2 tog, psso) 3 times, yf, k3; rep from * 7 times] 5 times.

ROUND 91 [* K1, yf, skpo, k1, k2 tog, yf, k4; rep from * 7 times in all] 5 times.

ROUND 93 [* K2, yf, sl 1, k2 tog, psso, yf, k3, yf, k1, yf, k1; rep from * 7 times in all] 5 times.

ROUND 95 [* K3, yf, k1, yf, k3, k2 tog, yf,

Knitted in the round, this filigree tablecloth displays petals, leaves and a feather and fan border.

k1, yf, skpo; rep from * 7 times] 5 times.

ROUND 97 Sl first st of next round onto end of last round then work as follows: [* K7, k2 tog, k1, yf, k1, yf, k1, skpo; rep from * 7 times in all] 5 times.

ROUND 99 Sl first st of next round onto end of last round then work as follows: [* K5, k2 tog, k2, yf, k1, yf, k2, skpo; rep from * 7 times in all] 5 times.

ROUND 101 Sl first st of next round onto end of last round then work as follows: [* K3, k2 tog, k3, yf, k1, yf, k3, skpo; rep from * 7 times in all] 5 times.

ROUND 103 Sl first st of next round onto end of last round then work as follows: [* K1, k2 tog, k4, yf, k1, yf, k4, skpo; rep from * 7 times in all] 5 times.

ROUND 105 Sl last st of last round onto beg of new round then work as follows: [* Sl 1, k2 tog, psso, yf, k5, yf, k1, yf, k5, yf; rep from * 7 times in all] 5 times.

ROUND 107 [* K2, yf, k6, yf, k1, yf, k6, yf, k1; rep from * 7 times in all] 5 times.

ROUND 109 Sl last st of last round onto beg of new round then work as follows: [* Yf, sl 1, k2 tog, psso, yf, k1B, yf, skpo, k11, k2 tog, yf, k1B; rep from * 7 times in all] 5 times.

ROUND 111 [* K1, yf, k1B, yf, k3, yf, k2 tog, k9, skpo, yf, k2; rep from * 7 times in all] 5 times. (770 sts).

ROUND 113 Sl first st of next round onto end of last round then work as follows: [* (Yf, sl 1, k2 tog, psso) twice, yf, k1B, yf, k2 tog, k7, skpo, yf, k1B, yf, sl 1, k2 tog, psso; rep from * 7 times] 5 times.

ROUND 115 [* Yf, k3, yf, k1B, yf, k3, yf, k2 tog, k5, skpo, yf, k3, yf, k1B; rep from * 7 times in all] 5 times.

ROUND 117 [* K1, sl 1, k2 tog, psso, k3, yf, sl 1, k2 tog, psso, yf, k1B, yf, k2 tog, k3, skpo, yf, k1B, yf, sl 1, k2 tog, psso, yf, k2; rep from * 7 times in all] 5 times.

ROUND 119 [* P3 tog, p2 tog, k1, yf, k1B, yf, k3, yf, k2 tog, k1, skpo, yf, k3, yf,

k1B, yf, k1, p2 tog; rep from * 7 times in all] 5 times.

ROUND 121 [K3, (sl 1, k2 tog, psso, yf) twice, k1B, yf, sl 1, k2 tog, psso, yf, k1B, (yf, sl 1, k2 tog, psso) twice, k2; rep from * 7 times in all] 5 times.

ROUND 123 [* K7, (yf, k1) twice, yf, inc 1, (yf, k1) twice, yf, k6; rep from * 7 times in all] 5 times.

ROUND 125 [* (P2 tog) twice, k4, (yf, k1) 4 times, yf, k2 tog, (yf, k1) 4 times, yf, k4, p2 tog, p1; rep from * 7 times in all] 5 times.

ROUND 127 Knit.

ROUND 129 Knit.

ROUND 131 [* (P2 tog) 4 times, (yf, k2 tog) 3 times, yf, k3 tog, (yf, k2 tog) 3 times, yf, (p2 tog) 4 times; rep from * 7 times in all] 5 times.

ROUND 133 Knit.

ROUND 135 Knit.

ROUND 137 [* (P2 tog) 4 times, (yf, k1) 7 times, yf, (p2 tog) 4 times; rep from * 7 times in all] 5 times.

ROUND 139 Knit.

ROUND 141 Knit.

ROUND 143 Work as round 137th.

ROUND 145 Knit.

ROUND 147 Knit.

ROUND 149 Work as round 137th.

ROUND 151 Knit.

ROUND 153 Knit.

ROUND 155 [* P2 tog, p1, p2 tog, p2, (yf, k1) 9 times, yf, p2, p2 tog, p1, p2 tog; rep from * 7 times in all] 5 times.

ROUND 157 Knit.

ROUND 159 Knit.

ROUND 161 [* (P2 tog) 5 times, (yf, k1) 9 times, yf, (p2 tog) 5 times; rep from * 7 times in all] 5 times.

ROUND 163 Knit.

ROUND 165 Knit.

ROUND 167 Work as round 161st.

ROUND 169 Knit.

ROUND 171 Knit.

ROUND 173 [* (P2 tog) twice, p1, (p2 tog)

twice, (yf, k1) 11 times, yf, (p2 tog) twice, p1, (p2 tog) twice; rep from * 7 times in all] 5 times.

ROUND 175 Knit.

ROUND 177 Knit.

ROUND 179 [* (P2 tog) 6 times, (yf, k1) 11 times, yf, (p2 tog) 6 times; rep from * 7 times in all] 5 times.

ROUND 181 Knit.

ROUND 183 Knit.

Using a crochet hook * (pick up 4 sts, yarn around hook through all 4 sts, yarn around hook, through both sts on hook, 11ch) rep from * all around, ss into top of first group. Fasten off.

Finishing the cloth

Working in sections, pin out the cloth to shape following the illustrated instructions given on page 102. Spray with water and allow each section to dry completely before removing the pins.

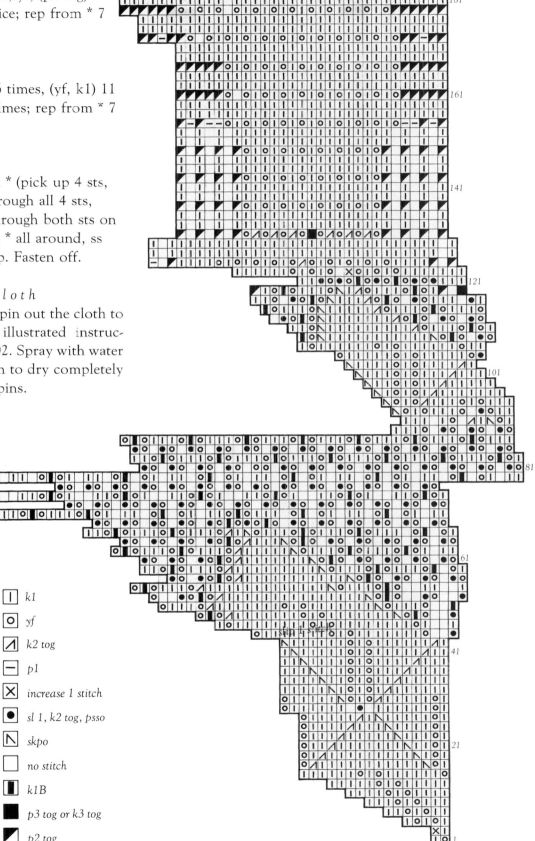

	k1
o	yf
⟋	k2 tog
−	p1
X	increase 1 stitch
●	sl 1, k2 tog, psso
N	skpo
	no stitch
▌	k1B
■	p3 tog or k3 tog
◢	p2 tog

WINDMILL MAT

Octagonal windmill motifs are joined together with two other shapes to make this delicate knitted mat which can be used on a dressing table or as a table centre. A deep edging, knitted separately and attached after all the motifs have been joined, completes the mat. The mat can be made larger or smaller, or the motifs and edging can be worked in heavier cotton to make a cot cover or bedspread.
Suitable for the experienced knitter, this design uses a variety of techniques including circular knitting on a set of double-pointed needles.

Materials
White cotton yarn, no 10 or finer
Pair of 2 mm knitting needles
Set of four 2 mm double-pointed needles
Sewing needle
Pins

Measurements
The mat is made from multiples of three different knitted shapes stitched together, plus a knitted lace edging. You can make the mat larger or smaller by adding or subtracting the relevant shapes.

Abbreviations
Knitting abbreviations appear on page 99. Special abbreviations for this pattern:
yf = yarn forward
skpo = slip 1 stitch, knit 1 stitch, pass slipped stitch over
sk2togpo = slip 1 stitch, knit 2 stitches together, pass slipped stitch over

Working the shapes
SHAPE A *(make 6)*
Using four needles, cast on 8 sts (3 sts on each of two needles and 2 sts on the third needle).
Join into a circle and work in rounds (page 98).
ROUND 1 Knit.
ROUND 2 * Yf, k1; rep from * to end.
ROUND 3 AND EVERY ALT ROUND Knit.
ROUND 4 * Yf, k2; rep from * to end.
ROUND 6 * Yf, k3; rep from * to end.
ROUND 8 * Yf, k4; rep from * to end.
ROUND 10 * Yf, k5; rep from * to end.
ROUND 12 * Yf, k6; rep from * to end.
ROUND 14 * Yf, k7; rep from * to end.
ROUND 16 * Yf, k8; rep from * to end.
ROUND 18 * Yf, k9; rep from * to end.
ROUND 20 * Yf, k10; rep from * to end.
ROUND 22 * Yf, k11; rep from * to end.
ROUND 24 * Yf, k1, yf, sl 1, k1, psso, k9; rep from * to end.
ROUND 26 * Yf, k1, yf, k2 tog, yf, sl 1, k1, psso, k8; rep from * to end.
ROUND 28 * Yf, k1, yf, [k2 tog, yf] twice, sl 1, k1, psso, k7; rep from * to end.
ROUND 30 * Yf, k1, yf, [k2 tog, yf] 3 times, sl 1 k1, psso, k6; rep from * to end.
ROUND 32 * Yf, k1, yf, [k2 tog, yf] 4 times, sl 1, k1, psso, k5; rep from * to end.
ROUND 34 * Yf, k1, yf, [k2 tog, yf] 5 times, sl 1, k1, psso, k4; rep from * to end.
ROUND 36 * Yf, k1, yf, [k2 tog, yf] 6 times, sl 1, k1, psso, k3; rep from * to end.
ROUND 38 * Yf, k1, yf, [k2 tog, yf] 7 times, sl 1, k1, psso, k2; rep from * to end.
ROUND 40 * Yf, k1, yf, [k2 tog, yf] 8 times, sl 1, k1, psso, k1; rep from * to end.
ROUND 42 * Yf, k1, yf, [k2 tog, yf] 9 times, sl 1, k1, psso; rep from * to end.

A series of windmill motifs makes a delightful and decorative mat for the dining or dressing table. The deep border is knitted separately and joined once the mat has been completed.

ROUND 43 Knit.
Cast off loosely knitwise until there are 22 sts left on the left-hand needle.

LINKING SQUARE
Change to the pair of needles and continue on these 22 sts, working backwards and forwards in rows as follows:
ROW 1 (RIGHT SIDE FACING) Sl 1, k to end.

ROW 2 Sl 1, p to end.
ROW 3 Sl 1, k to end.
Repeat these 3 rows 12 times more.
NEXT ROW Sl 1, k to end.
NEXT ROW Sl 1, p to end.
Cast off loosely knitwise.

SHAPE B (make 6)
Work as for shape A until round 43 is complete. Cast off all sts loosely knitwise.

SHAPE C (make 6)

Using pair of needles, cast on 22 sts.

ROW 1 (RIGHT SIDE FACING) Sl 1, k to end.

ROW 2 Sl 1, p to end.

ROW 3 Sl 1, k to last 2 sts, k2 tog.

Repeat these 3 rows for the pattern, **at the same time**, decrease one st at end of every right side row until 2 sts remain.

NEXT ROW K2 tog and fasten off.

Joining the shapes

1 Sew in the ends. Pin out the shapes following the illustrated instructions on page 102, making sure that all the hexagon, square and triangular shapes are the same size. Spray lightly with water and allow to dry completely.

2 Using the diagram below as a guide, stitch the shapes together using one of the methods shown on page 102. When complete, press the mat lightly.

Working the edging

Cast on 33 sts.

ROW 1 (RIGHT SIDE FACING) Sl 1, k2, yf, k2 tog, yf, K5, yf, sk2togpo, yf, k5, yf, k2 tog, yf, k1, [yf, k2 tog] 5 times, yf, k2.

ROW 2 K14, p17, k2, yf, k2 tog, k1.

ROW 3 Sl 1, k2, yf, k2 tog, yf, k1, k2 tog, p1, skpo, k1, p1, k1, k2 tog, p1, skpo, k1, yf, k2 tog, yf, k2, [yf, k2 tog] 5 times, yf, k2.

ROW 4 K15, p5, [k1, p2] twice, k1, p3, k2, yf, k2 tog, k1.

ROW 5 Sl 1, k2, yf, k2 tog, yf, k1, yf, k2 tog, p1, skpo, p1, k2 tog, p1, skpo, yf, k1, yf, k2 tog, yf, k3, [yf, k2 tog] 5 times, yf, k2.

ROW 6 K16, p6, k1, [p1, k1] twice, p4, k2, yf, k2 tog, k1.

ROW 7 Sl 1, k2, yf, k2 tog, yf, k3, yf, sk2togpo, p1, k3 tog, yf, k3, yf, k2 tog, yf, k4, [yf, k2 tog] 5 times, yf, k2.

ROW 8 K17, p15, k2, yf, k2 tog, k1.

ROW 9 Sl 1, k2, yf, k2 tog, yf, k5, yf, sk2togpo, yf, k5, yf, k2 tog, yf, k5, [yf, k2 tog] 5 times, yf, k2.

ROW 10 K18, p17, k2, yf, k2 tog, k1.

ROW 11 Sl 1, k2, yf, k2 tog, yf, k1, k2 tog, p1, skpo, k1, p1, k1, k2 tog, p1, skpo, k1, yf, k2 tog, yf, k6, [yf, k2 tog] 5 times, yf, k2.

ROW 12 K19, p5, [k1, p2] twice, k1, p3, k2, yf, k2 tog, k1.

ROW 13 Sl 1, k2, yf, k2 tog, yf, k1, yf, k2 tog, p1, skpo, p1, k2 tog, p1, skpo, yf, k1, yf, k2 tog, yf, k7, [yf, k2 tog] 5 times, yf, k2.

ROW 14 K20, p6, k1, [p1, k1] twice, p4, k2, yf, k2 tog, k1.

ROW 15 Sl 1, k2, yf, k2 tog, yf, k3, yf, sk2togpo, p1, k3 tog, yf, k3, yf, k2 tog, yf, k8, [yf, k2 tog] 5 times, yf, k2.

ROW 16 K21, p15, k2, yf, k2 tog, k1.

ROW 17 Sl 1, k2, yf, k2 tog, yf, k5, sk2togpo, yf, k5, yf, k2 tog, yf, k9, [yf, k2 tog] 5 times, yf, k2.

ROW 18 K22, p17, k2, yf, k2 tog, k1.

ROW 19 Sl 1, k2, yf, k2 tog, yf, k1, k2 tog, p1, skpo, k1, p1, k1, k2 tog, p1, skpo, k1, yf, k2 tog, yf, k10, [yf, k2 tog] 5 times, yf, k2.

ROW 20 K23, p5, [k1, p2] twice, k1, p3, k2, yf, k2 tog, k1.

ROW 21 Sl 1, k2, yf, k2 tog, yf, k1, yf, k2 tog, p1, skpo, p1, k2 tog, p1, skpo, yf, k1, yf, k2 tog, yf, k11, [yf, k2 tog] 5 times, yf, k2.

ROW 22 K24, p6, k1, [p1, k1] twice, p4, k2, yf, k2 tog, k1.

ROW 23 Sl 1, k2, yf, k2 tog, yf, k3, yf, sk2togpo, p1, k3 tog, yf, k3, yf, k2 tog, yf, k12, [yf, k2 tog] 5 times, yf, k2.

ROW 24 Cast off 12 sts loosely knitwise, k next 12 sts, p15, k2, yf, k2 tog, k1. (33 sts)

Repeat rows 1 to 24 until the edging is long enough to go round the outer edge of the mat, ending with a 24th row and allowing a little extra edging at each corner so it will lie flat when attached.

Applying the edging

1 Sew in the ends. Pin out the edging following the illustrated instructions given on page 102. Spray lightly with water and allow to dry thoroughly.

2 Pin the edging around the mat making sure you space out the points evenly and that you gather the corners to fit. Oversew the edging in place, taking care not to pull the stitches tight. Carefully sew together the cast-on and cast-off sides of the edging.

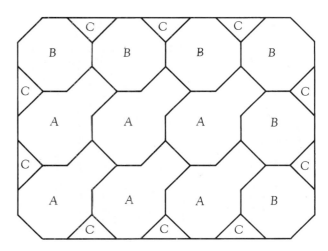

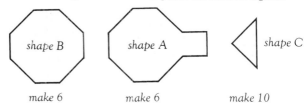

Diagram to show how pieces are stitched together

shape B — make 6
shape A — make 6
shape C — make 10

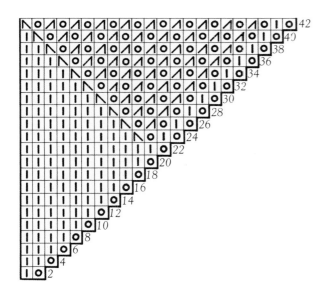

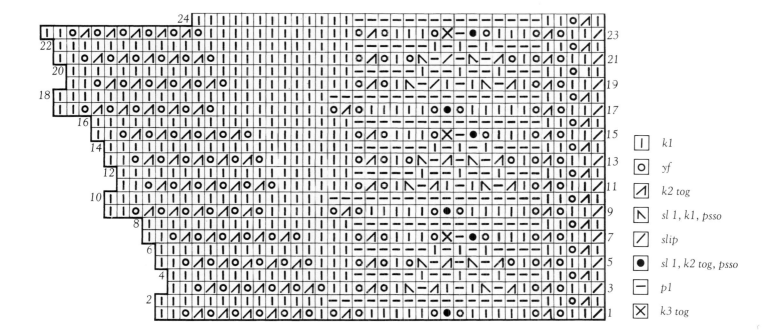

I	k1
O	yf
⊿	k2 tog
⊼	sl 1, k1, psso
⁄	slip
●	sl 1, k2 tog, psso
–	p1
⊠	k3 tog

SCANDINAVIAN
TOWEL

A deep, knitted border complements this cream towel perfectly and it would be easy to decorate all your towels in the same way. Work the same pattern in fine cotton to make narrower edging for face flannels, guest towels and a towelling robe. When working the border, take care to finish the knitting at the end of one complete pattern repeat to make sure that the design at each end of the strip is perfectly symmetrical. Instructions for two more deep border designs are given on page 143.

Materials
Cream double knitting weight cotton
Cream towel
Pair of 3.5 mm knitting needles
Matching sewing thread
Sewing needle
Pins
Starch (optional)

Measurements
Each pattern repeat measures approximately 8 cm (3 in) and seven pattern repeats were needed to edge the hand towel shown here. To edge a larger towel, work further complete pattern repeats until you reach the desired length.

Abbreviations
Knitting abbreviations appear on page 99.

Working the edging
Cast on 16 sts and knit 1 row.
ROW 1 Yo, k2 tog, k1, yo, k10, yo, k2 tog, k1.

ROW 2 K2, yo, k2 tog, k12, p1.
ROW 3 Yo, k2 tog, k1, yo, k2 tog, yo, k9, yo, k2 tog, k1.
ROW 4 K2, yo, k2 tog, k13, p1.
ROW 5 Yo, k2 tog, k1, [yo, k2 tog] twice, yo, k8, yo, k2 tog, k1.
ROW 6 K2, yo, k2 tog, k14, p1.
ROW 7 Yo, k2 tog, k1, [yo, k2 tog] 3 times, yo, k7, yo, k2 tog, k1.
ROW 8 K2, yo, k2 tog, k15, p1.
ROW 9 Yo, k2 tog, k1, [yo, k2 tog] 4 times, yo, k6, yo, k2 tog, k1.
ROW 10 K2, yo, k2 tog, k16, p1.
ROW 11 Yo, k2 tog, k1, [yo, k2 tog] 5 times, yo, k5, yo, k2 tog, k1.
ROW 12 K2, yo, k2 tog, k17, p1.
ROW 13 Yo, k2 tog, k1, [yo, k2 tog] 6 times, yo, k4, yo, k2 tog, k1.
ROW 14 K2, yo, k2 tog, k18, p1.
ROW 15 Yo, k2 tog, k1, [yo, k2 tog] 7 times, yo, k3, yo, k2 tog, k1.
ROW 16 K2, yo, k2 tog, k19, p1.
ROW 17 Yo, [k2 tog] twice, [yo, k2 tog] 7 times, k3, yo, k2 tog, k1.
ROW 18 Rep row 14.
ROW 19 Yo, [k2 tog] twice, [yo, k2 tog] 6 times, k4, yo, k2 tog, k1.
ROW 20 Rep row 12.
ROW 21 Yo, [k2 tog] twice, [yo, k2 tog] 5 times, k5, yo, k2 tog, k1.
ROW 22 Rep row 10.
ROW 23 Yo, [k2 tog] twice, [yo, k2 tog] 4 times, k6, yo, k2 tog, k1.
ROW 24 Rep row 8.
ROW 25 Yo, [k2 tog] twice, [yo, k2 tog] 3 times, k7, yo, k2 tog, k1.
ROW 26 Rep row 6.
ROW 27 Yo, [k2 tog] twice, [yo, k2 tog] twice, k8, yo, k2 tog, k1.
ROW 28 Rep row 4.
ROW 29 Yo, [k2 tog] twice, yo, k2 tog, k9, yo, k2 tog, k1.
ROW 30 Rep row 2.
ROW 31 Yo, [k2 tog] twice, k10, yo, k2 tog, k1.
ROW 32 K2, yo, k2 tog, k11, p1.

Attractive edgings turn plain towels into heirloom pieces perfect for a wedding or anniversary gift. Make a more delicate border for guest towels or face cloths using a finer weight cotton.

Repeat rows 1 to 32 until the edging is the required length, ending with a 32nd row.

Cast off loosely knitwise.

Applying the edging

1 Sew in the ends. Pin out the edging following the illustrated instructions given on page 102. Spray with water and allow to dry completely before removing the pins. For a starched finish, choose a soft-finish starch and apply it following the manufacturer's instruction before pinning out.

2 Pin the edging along one short edge of the towel, making sure you space out the points evenly. Oversew the edging in place with matching sewing thread, taking care not to pull the stitches tight.

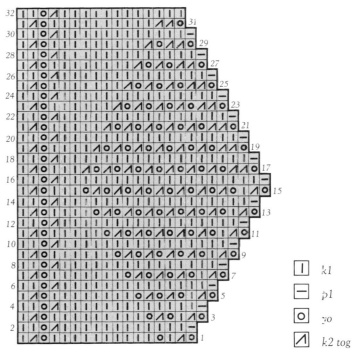

	k1
-	p1
o	yo
/\	k2 tog

VICTORIAN BEDSPREAD

Knit this Victorian-style bedspread in heavy white cotton yarn and create a wonderful heirloom which can be enjoyed by you and your family for many years to come. The bedspread is knitted in squares and you will need to make four of the following motifs to complete one whole pattern. The motifs are stitched together after pinning out and blocking, then the simple ribbed edging is attached.

When laundering the bedspread, allow it to dry naturally away from sunlight and artificial heat. If necessary, press the bedspread lightly on the wrong side with a warm iron over a well-padded surface, taking care not to crush the raised leaf shapes. Check the seams over periodically to make sure that none of the stitching has worked loose and make repairs as soon as possible.

When storing the bedspread for long periods of time, first make sure that it is perfectly clean and dry, then wrap it in white, acid-free tissue paper and store it in a cool and dry place.

Materials
White cotton yarn approx 3 to 4 ply
Pair of 3.25 mm knitting needles
Tapestry needle
Pins

Measurements
Each square motif measures approximately 15 cm (6 in) on the original bedspread and the complete pattern is made up of four motifs arranged so that four single leaves touch at the centre. The double size bedspread shown here is made from 168 motifs joined in 12 strips of 14 motifs and the edging is knitted in four overlapping sections. Begin by knitting one complete repeat of the pattern, measure the resulting square motif and then calculate how many squares you will need to knit to make a spread the right size to fit your bed.

Abbreviations
Knitting abbreviations appear on page 99.
Special abbreviations for this pattern:
yf = yarn forward
inc = knit into the front and then the back of the next stitch

Working the motif (make 168)
Place a loop on the needle.
Knit into the front, back and then front of this loop – 3 sts made.
Now proceed as follows:
ROW 1 (RIGHT SIDE FACING) K1, [yf, k1] twice.
ROW 2 Inc in first st, p3, inc in last st.
ROW 3 K3, yf, k1, yf, k3.
ROW 4 Inc in first st, k1, p5, k1, inc in last st.
ROW 5 K5, yf, k1, yf, k5.
ROW 6 Inc in first st, k2, p7, k2, inc in last st.
ROW 7 K7, yf, k1, yf, k7.
ROW 8 Inc in first st, k3, p9, k3, inc in last st.

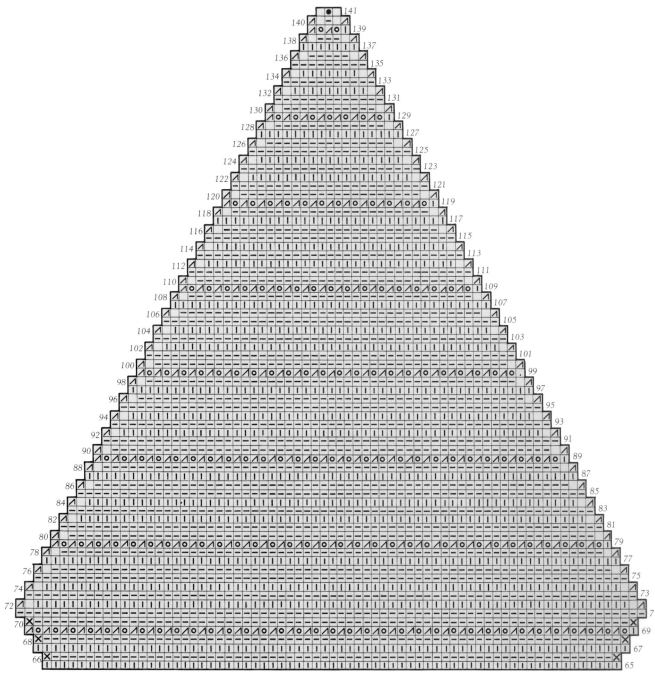

Chart for eyelet pattern

Chart for border

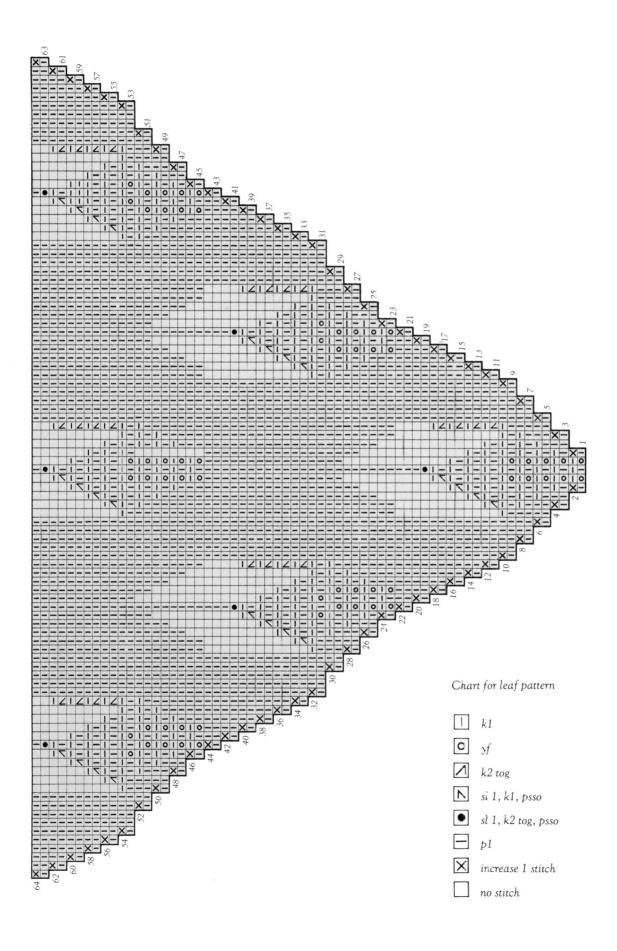

Chart for leaf pattern

| | k1

| o | yf

| ⟋ | k2 tog

| ⟍ | sl 1, k1, psso

| • | sl 1, k2 tog, psso

| − | p1

| ✕ | increase 1 stitch

| | no stitch

ROW 9 K9, yf, k1, yf, k9.

ROW 10 Inc in first st, k4, p11, k4, inc in last st.

ROW 11 K6, sl 1, k1, psso, k7, k2 tog, k6.

ROW 12 Inc in first st, k5, p9, k5, inc in last st.

ROW 13 K7, sl 1, k1, psso, k5, k2 tog, k7.

ROW 14 Inc in first st, k6, p7, k6, inc in last st.

ROW 15 K8, sl 1, k1, psso, k3, k2 tog, k8.

ROW 16 Inc in first st, k7, p5, k7, inc in last st.

ROW 17 K9, sl 1, k1, psso, k1, k2 tog, k9.

ROW 18 Inc in first st, k8, p3, k8, inc in last st.

ROW 19 K10, sl 1, k2 tog, psso, k10.

ROW 20 Inc in first st, k19, inc in last st.

ROW 21 K23.

ROW 22 Inc in first st, k21, inc in last st (25 sts).

ROW 23 [K1, yf] twice, k21, [yf, k1] twice.

ROW 24 Inc in first st, p3, k21, p3, inc in last st.

ROW 25 K3, yf, k1, k23, yf, k1, yf, k3.

ROW 26 Inc in first st, k1, p5, k21, p5, k1, inc in last st.

ROW 27 K5, yf, k1, yf, k25, yf, k1, yf, k5.

ROW 28 Inc in first st, k2, p7, k21, p7, k2, inc in last st.

ROW 29 K7, yf, k1, yf, k27, yf, k1, yf, k7.

ROW 30 Inc in first st, k3, p9, k21, p9, k3, inc in last st.

ROW 31 K9, yf, k1, yf, k29, yf, k1, yf, k9.

ROW 32 Inc in first st, k4, p11, k21, p11, k4, inc in last st.

ROW 33 K6, sl 1, k1, psso, k7, k2 tog, k21, sl 1, k1, psso, k7, k2 tog, k6.

ROW 34 Inc in first st, k5, p9, k21, p9, k5, inc in last st.

ROW 35 K7, sl 1, k1, psso, k5, k2 tog, k21, sl 1, k1, psso, k5, k2 tog, k7.

ROW 36 Inc in first st, k6, p7, k21, p7, k6, inc in last st.

ROW 37 K8, sl 1, k1, psso, k3, k2 tog, k21, sl 1, k1, psso, k3, k2 tog, k8.

ROW 38 Inc in first st, k7, p5, k21, p5,

ROW 39 K9, sl 1, k1, psso, k1, k2 tog, k21, sl 1, k1, psso, k1, k2 tog, k9.

ROW 40 Inc in first st, k8, p3, k21, p3, k8, inc in last st.

ROW 41 K10, sl 1, k2 tog, psso, k21, sl 1, k2 tog, psso, k10.

ROW 42 Inc in first st, k41, inc in last st.

ROW 43 K45.

ROW 44 Inc in first st, k43, inc in last st (47 sts).

ROW 45 K1, [yf, k1, yf, k21] twice, yf, k1, yf, k1.

ROW 46 Inc in first st, [p3, k21] twice, p3, inc in last st.

ROW 47 K3, [yf, k1, yf, k23] twice, yf, k1, yf, k3.

ROW 48 Inc in first st, k1, [p5, k21] twice, p5, k1, inc in last st.

ROW 49 K5, [yf, k1, yf, k25] twice, yf, k1, yf, k5.

ROW 50 Inc in first st, k2, [p7, k21] twice, p7, k2, inc in last st.

ROW 51 K7, [yf, k1, yf, k27] twice, yf, k1, yf, k7.

ROW 52 Inc in first st, k3, [p9, k21] twice, p9, k3, inc in last st.

ROW 53 K9, [yf, k1, yf, k29] twice, yf, k1, yf, k9.

ROW 54 Inc in first st, k4, [p11, k21] twice, p11, k4, inc in last st.

ROW 55 K6, [sl 1, k1, psso, k7, k2 tog, k21] twice, sl 1, k1, psso, k7, k2 tog, k6.

ROW 56 Inc in first st, k5, [p9, k21] twice, p9, k5, inc in last st.

ROW 57 K7, [sl 1, k1, psso, k2 tog, k21] twice, sl 1, k1, psso, k5, k2 tog, k7.

ROW 58 Inc in first st, k6, [p7, k21] twice, p7, k6, inc in last st.

ROW 59 K8, [sl 1, k1, psso, k3, k2 tog, k21] twice, sl 1, k1, psso, k3, k2 tog, k8.

ROW 60 Inc in first st, k7, [p5, k21] twice, p5, k7, inc in last st.

ROW 61 K9, [sl 1, k1, psso, k1, k2 tog, k21] twice, sl 1, k1, psso, k1, k2 tog, k9.

ROW 62 Inc in first st, k8, [p8, k21] twice,

k7, inc in last st.

p3, k8, inc in last st.

ROW 63 K10, [sl 1, k2 tog, psso, k21] twice, sl 1, k2 tog, psso, k10.

ROW 64 Inc in first st, k63, inc in last st.

Now begin eyelet pattern:

ROW 65 (RIGHT SIDE FACING) K67.

ROW 66 Inc in first st, p to last st, inc in last st.

ROW 67 Knit.

ROW 68 Inc in first st, p to last st, inc in last st.

ROW 69 K1, [yf, k2 tog] to end.

ROW 70 Inc in first st, p to last st, inc in last st

(73 sts)

**ROW 71 Purl.

ROW 72 K2 tog, k to last 2 sts, k2 tog.

ROW 73 Purl.

ROW 74 K2 tog, k to last 2 sts, k2 tog.

ROW 75 Purl.

ROW 76 K2 tog, p to last 2 sts, k2 tog.

ROW 77 Knit.

ROW 78 K2 tog, p to last 2 sts, k2 tog.

ROW 79 K1, [yf, k2 tog] to end.

ROW 80 K2 tog, p to last 2 sts, k2 tog. **

Rep the 10 rows between ** and ** 6 times more – 3 sts remain.

NEXT ROW S1, k2 tog, psso.

Fasten off.

Working the border
Border for longer edge (make 2):

Cast on 33 sts

ROW 1 (RIGHT SIDE FACING) Purl.

ROW 2 Knit.

ROWS 3 AND 4 Rep rows 1 and 2.

ROWS 5, 6 AND 8 Purl.

ROW 7 Knit.

ROW 9 K2, [yf, k2 tog] to last st, k1.

ROW 10 Purl.

Rep these 10 rows until border, when slightly stretched, fits along one longer edge of the bedspread, ending with a 5th pattern row. Cast off.

Border for shorter edge (make 2):
Work as for longer edge of border, but

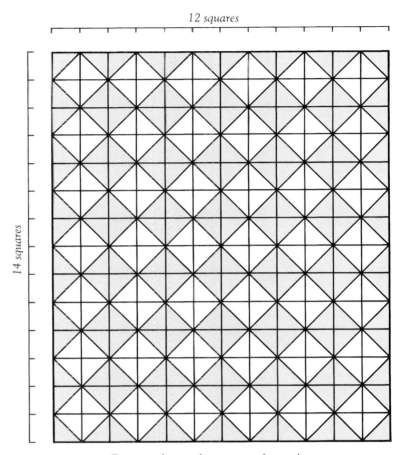

12 squares

14 squares

Diagram showing how squares fit together

rep the 10 rows until border, when slightly stretched, fits along one shorter edge of the bedspread, including cast-on and cast-off edges of longer borders, ending with a 5th pattern row.
Cast off.

Making up the bedspread
1 Pin out each motif to the same size, following the illustrated instructions on page 102. Spray with water and allow each motif to dry completely before removing the pins.
2 Stitch the motifs together following the diagram on page 102.
3 Sew the borders in place along the longer edges of the bedspread, then attach the shorter borders.

Pattern Library

LACE EDGINGS

These four edgings can all be worked in heavy, double knitting weight cotton yarn to decorate towels or knitted bedspreads. If you prefer, the three lacy edgings can have a more delicate appearance by simply substituting finer thread and needles.

The designs are knitted vertically and can be stitched to woven fabrics or a piece of knitting.

Abbreviations
Knitting abbreviations appear on page 99.

ZIGZAG EDGING (green)
Cast on 8 sts and knit 1 row.
ROW 1 Sl 1, k1, [yo, k2 tog] twice, yo, k2.
ROWS 2, 4, 6 AND 8 Sl 1, knit to end of row.
ROW 3 Sl 1, k2, [yo, k2 tog] twice, yo, k2.
ROW 5 Sl 1, k3, [yo, k2 tog] twice, yo, k2.
ROW 7 Sl 1, k4, [yo, k2 tog] twice, yo, k2.
ROW 9 Sl 1, k11.
ROW 10 Cast off 4 sts, knit to end of row.
Repeat rows 1 to 10.

SAWTOOTH EDGING (peach)

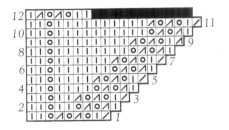

Cast on 8 sts and knit 1 row.
ROW 1 Sl 1, k1, [yo, k2 tog] twice, yo, k2.
ROW 2 K2, yo, k2, [yo, k2 tog] twice, k1.
ROW 3 Sl 1, k1, [yo, k2 tog] twice, k2, yo, k2.
ROW 4 K2, yo, k4, [yo, k2 tog] twice, k1.
ROW 5 Sl 1, k1, [yo, k2 tog] twice, k4, yo, k2.
ROW 6 K2, yo, k6, [yo, k2 tog] twice, k1.
ROW 7 Sl 1, k1, [yo, k2 tog] twice, k6, yo, k2.
ROW 8 K2, yo, k8, [yo, k2 tog] twice, k1.
ROW 9 Sl 1, k1, [yo, k2 tog] twice, k8, yo, k2.
ROW 10 K2, yo, k10, [yo, k2 tog] twice, k1.
ROW 11 Sl 1, k1, [yo, k2 tog] twice, k10, yo, k2.
ROW 12 Cast off 11 sts, k2, [yo, k2 tog] twice, k1.
Repeat rows 1 to 12.

KNIT AND PURL EDGING (blue)

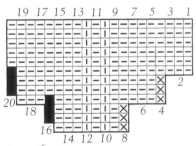

Cast on 6 sts.
ROWS 1, 2 AND 3 Knit.
ROW 4 Cast on 3 sts, knit to end of row.
ROWS 5, 6 AND 7 Knit.
ROW 8 Cast on 3 sts, knit to end of row.
ROWS 9 AND 11 Knit.
ROWS 10 AND 12 Purl.

ROWS 13, 14 AND 15 Knit.

ROW 16 Cast off 3 sts, knit to end of row.

ROWS 17, 18 AND 19 Knit.

ROW 20 Cast off 3 sts, knit to end of row.
Repeat rows 1 to 20.

SCALLOPED TRELLIS EDGING (cream)

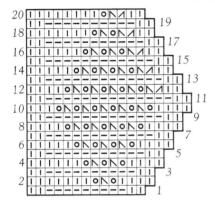

Cast on 13 sts.

ROW 1 AND EVERY ALTERNATE ROW K2, purl to last 2 sts, k2.

ROW 2 K7, yo, sl 1, k1, psso, yo, k4.

ROW 4 K6, [yo, sl 1, k1, psso] twice, yo, k4.

ROW 6 K5, [yo, sl 1, k1, psso] 3 times, yo, k4.

ROW 8 K4, [yo, sl 1, k1, psso] 4 times, yo, k4.

ROW 10 K3, [yo, sl 1, k1, psso] 5 times, yo, k4.

ROW 12 K4, [yo, sl 1, k1, psso] 5 times, k2 tog, k2.

ROW 14 K5, [yo, sl 1, k1, psso] 4 times, k2 tog, k2.

ROW 16 K6, [yo, sl 1, k1, psso] 3 times, k2 tog, k2.

ROW 18 K7, [yo, sl 1, k1, psso] twice, k2 tog, k2.

ROW 20 K8, yo, sl 1, k1, psso, k2 tog, k2.
Repeat rows 1 to 20.

LACE BORDERS

Abbreviations
Knitting abbreviations appear on page 99.
Special abbreviation for Continental:
inc = knit and purl into the next stitch.

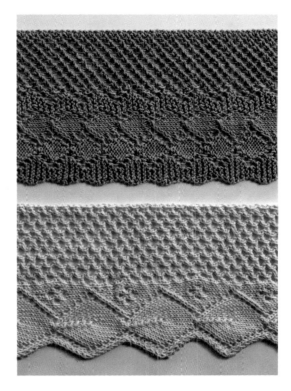

Both the designs shown on this page are quite a challenge to knit, but understanding the pattern will become easier once the first complete repeat of each design has been worked. Take special care to work the increase on the Continental border design as described in the Abbreviations section, as a completely different effect is produced if the increase is worked by the more usual method.

DIAMOND AND LACE BORDER (blue)

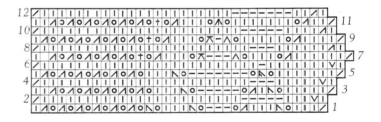

Cast on 34 sts and knit one row.

ROW 1 Sl 1, k3, yo, sl 1, k1, psso, k3, k2 tog, yo, p3, yo, sl 1, k1, psso, k3, yo, sl 1, k1, psso, [yo, k2 tog] 6 times, k1.

ROW 2 Sl 1, k23, p5, k3, [k1, p1] in next st, k1.

ROW 3 Sl 1, k5, yo, sl 1, k1, psso, k1, k2 tog, yo, p5, yo, sl 1, k1, psso, k3, [yo, k2 tog] 6 times, k2.

ROW 4 Sl 1, k24, p3, k5, [k1, p1] in next st, k1.

ROW 5 Sl 1, k7, yo, sl 1, k2 tog, psso, yo, p7, yo, sl 1, k1, psso, k3, [yo, k2 tog] 6 times, k1.

ROW 6 Sl 1, k25, p1, k7, [k1, p1] in next st, k1.

	k1
⟋	k2 tog
✝	k1 tbl
⟍	sl 1, k1, psso
⟍	sl 1, k2 tog, psso
–	p1
⋀	p2 tog
⊼	p2 tog tbl
⋀	p3 tog
⋁	[k1, p1] in next stitch
✕	cast on 1 stitch
■	cast off 1 stitch
o	yo

ROW 7 Sl 1, k6, k2 tog, yo, k3, yo, p2 tog, p3, p2 tog tbl, yo, k3, k2 tog, yo, k1 tbl, [yo, k2 tog] 5 times, k2.
ROW 8 Sl 1, k24, p3, k6, k2 tog, k1.
ROW 9 Sl 1, k4, k2 tog, yo, k5, yo, p2 tog, p1, p2 tog tbl, yo, k3, k2 tog, yo, k1 tbl, [yo, k2 tog] 6 times, k1.
ROW 10 Sl 1, k23, p5, k4, k2 tog, k1.
ROW 11 Sl 1, k2, k2 tog, yo, k7, yo, p3 tog, yo, k3, k2 tog, yo, k1 tbl, [yo, k2 tog] 6 times, k2.
ROW 12 Sl 1, k22, p7, k2, k2 tog, k1.
Repeat rows 1 to 12.

CONTINENTAL BORDER (*peach*)

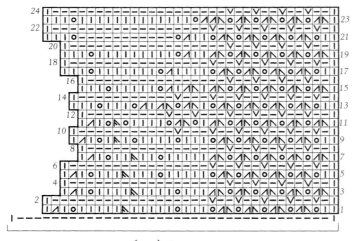

foundation row

	k1
	p1
o	yo
	k2 tog
	sl 1, k1, psso
	sl 1, k2 tog, psso
v	inc
	k2 tog tbl

Cast on 38 sts.
FOUNDATION ROW K1, p36, k1.
ROW 1 K2, [yo, sl 1, k1, psso, k2 tog] 4 times, yo, k3, yo, k5, sl 1, k2 tog, psso, k5, yo, k1, k2 tog, k1.
ROW 2 K1, p18, inc, [p2, inc] 4 times, p1, k1.
ROW 3 K1, [sl 1, k1, psso, k2 tog, yo] 4 times, sl 1, k1, psso, k2 tog, k3, yo, k4, sl 1, k2 tog, psso, k4, yo, k1, k2 tog, k1.
ROW 4 K1, p18, [inc, p2] 4 times, k1.
ROW 5 K2, [yo, sl 1, k1, psso, k2 tog] 4 times, yo, k5, yo, k3, sl 1, k2 tog, psso, k3, yo, k1, k2 tog, k1.
ROW 6 K1, p16, [inc, p2] 4 times, inc, p1, k1.

ROW 7 K1, [sl 1, k1, psso, k2 tog, yo] 4 times, sl 1, k1, psso, k2 tog, k5, yo, k2, sl 1, k2 tog, psso, k2, yo, k1, k2 tog, k1.
ROW 8 K1, p16, [inc, p2] 4 times, k1.
ROW 9 K2, [yo, sl 1, k1, psso, k2 tog] 4 times, yo, k3, yo, k4, yo, k1, sl 1, k2 tog, psso, k1, yo, k1, k2 tog, k1.
ROW 10 K1, p11, inc, p3, [inc, p2] 4 times, inc, p1, k1.
ROW 11 K1, [sl 1, k1, psso, k2 tog, yo] 4 times, sl 1, k1, psso, k2 tog, k1, yo, sl 1, k1, psso, k2 tog, yo, k4, yo, sl 1, k2 tog, psso, yo, k1, k2 tog, k1.
ROW 12 K1, p9, inc, p2, inc, p3, [inc, p2] 4 times, k1.
ROW 13 K2, [yo, sl 1, k1, psso, k2 tog] 4 times, yo, k1, sl 1, k1, psso, k2 tog, yo, sl 1, k1, psso, k2 tog, k1, k2 tog, yo, k3, yo, k3.
ROW 14 Rep row 10.
ROW 15 K1, [sl 1, k1, psso, k2 tog, yo] 4 times, sl 1, k1, psso, k2 tog, k1, sl 1, k1, psso, k2 tog, k1, k2 tog, yo, k5, yo, k3.
ROW 16 Rep row 8.
ROW 17 K2, [yo, sl 1, k1, psso, k2 tog] 4 times, yo, k4, k2 tog, yo, k7, yo, k3.
ROW 18 Rep row 6.
ROW 19 K1, [sl 1, k1, psso, k2 tog, yo] 4 times, sl 1, k1, psso, k2 tog, k2, k2 tog, yo, k9, yo, k3.
ROW 20 Rep row 4.
ROW 21 K2, [yo, sl 1, k1, psso, k2 tog] 4 times, yo, k2, k2 tog, yo, k11, yo, k3.
ROW 22 Rep row 2.
ROW 23 K1, [sl 1, k1, psso, k2 tog, yo] 4 times, sl 1, k1, psso, [k2 tog] twice, yo, k13, yo, k3.
ROW 24 K1, p20, [inc, p2] 4 times, k1.
Repeat rows 1 to 24.

LACE INSERTIONS

Abbreviations
A full list of knitting abbreviations are given on page 99.

Knitted lace insertions are very useful – an insertion can be worked in fine yarn and the resulting lace strip positioned between two pieces of fabric to provide a decorative feature on plain items. An insertion can also serve as an edging or be worked directly into a piece by knitting the pattern repeat in a central panel surrounded by plain panels.

NARROW INSERTION (cream)

Cast on 12 sts.

ROW 1 K3, yo, k2 tog, p2, k1, yo, k2 tog, k2.

ROW 2 K3, yo, k2 tog tbl, k3, yo, k2 tog tbl, k2.

Repeat rows 1 and 2.

ARROW INSERTION (beige)

Cast on 21 sts.

ROW 1 K3, yo, k2 tog, p2, yo, sl 1, k1, psso, k3, k2 tog, yo, p2, k1, yo, k2 tog, k2.

ROWS 2 AND 4 K3, yo, k2 tog tbl, k2, p7, k3, yo, k2 tog tbl, k2.

ROW 3 K3, yo, k2 tog, p2, k1, yo, sl 1, k1, psso, k1, k2 tog, yo, k1, p2, k1, yo,

k2 tog, k2.

ROW 5 K3, yo, k2 tog, p2, k2, yo, sl 1, k2 tog, psso, yo, k2, p2, k1, yo, k2 tog, k2.

ROW 6 K3, yo, k2 tog tbl, k2, p7, k3, yo, k2 tog tbl, k2. Repeat rows 1 to 6.

SINGLE HOLE INSERTION (blue)

Cast on 11 sts.

ROW 1 K2, p2, k1, yo, k2 tog, p2, k2.

ROW 2 K4, p3, k4.

ROW 3 Knit.

ROW 4 K2, p7, k2.

Repeat rows 1 to 4.

LEAF VEIN INSERTION (green)

Cast on 18 sts.

ROW 1 K3, k2 tog, yo, k5, yo, k3, sl 1, k1, psso, k3.

ROW 2 AND EVERY ALTERNATE ROW K3, p12, k3.

ROW 3 K3, k2 tog, k5, yo, k1, yo, k2, sl 1, k1, psso, k3.

ROW 5 K3, k2 tog, k4, yo, k3, yo, k1, sl 1, k1, psso, k3.

ROW 7 K3, k2 tog, k3, yo, k5, yo, sl 1, k1, psso, k3.

ROW 9 K3, k2 tog, k2, yo, k1, yo, k5, sl 1, k1, psso, k3.

ROW 11 K3, k2 tog, k1, yo, k3, yo, k4, sl 1, k1, psso, k3.

ROW 12 K3, p12, k3.

Repeat rows 1 to 12.

For the more experienced knitter, the two large lace patterns shown here are rewarding to knit. Work the leaf pattern (green) in fine wool synthetic yarn to make lacy garments, scarves and wraps, or knit several wide strips in heavy cotton and join them together to make an unusual bedspread.

LARGE LACE PATTERNS

Abbreviations

Knitting abbreviations appear on page 99. Special abbreviation for lace leaves:
inc = knit once into the front and once into the back of the next st.
Abbreviation for cathedral window:
yb = return yarn to back of work before working next stitch.

LACE LEAVES (green)

multiple of 19 sts + 1

Cast on a multiple of 19 sts plus 2.
ROWS 1, 3, 5 AND 7 K1, * sl 1, k1, psso, k3, [yo, sl 1, k1, psso] twice, yo, k1, yo, [k2 tog, yo] twice, k3, k2 tog; rep from * to last st, k1.
ROW 2 AND EVERY ALT ROW Purl.

ROW 9 K1, * sl 1, k1, psso, k2, [yo, k2 tog] twice, yo, k3, yo, [sl 1, k1, psso, yo] twice, k2, k2 tog; rep from * to last st, k1.
ROW 11 K1, * sl 1, k1, psso, k1, [yo, k2 tog] twice, yo, k5, yo, [sl 1, k1, psso, yo] twice, k1, k2 tog; rep from * to last st, k1.
ROW 13 K1, * sl 1, k1, psso, [yo, k2 tog] twice, yo, k7, yo, [sl 1, k1, psso, yo] twice, k2 tog; rep from * to last st, inc.
ROW 15 Sl 1, * k1, psso, [yo, k2 tog] twice, yo, k3, k2 tog, k4, yo, [sl 1, k1, psso, yo] twice, sl 1; rep from * to last 2 sts, k1, psso, k1.
ROWS 17, 19, 21 AND 23 K1, * [yo, k2 tog] twice, yo, k3, k2 tog, sl 1, k1, psso, k3, yo [sl 1, k1, psso, yo] twice, k1; rep from * to last st, k1.
ROW 25 K1, * k1, [yo, sl 1, k1, psso] twice, yo, k2, k2 tog, sl 1, k1, psso, k2, [yo, k2 tog] twice, yo, k2; rep from * to last st, k1.
ROW 27 K1, * k2, [yo, sl 1, k1, psso] twice, yo, k1, k2 tog, sl 1, k1, psso, k1, yo, [k2 tog, yo] twice, k3; rep from * to last st, k1.
ROW 29 K1, * k3, [yo, sl 1, k1, psso] twice, yo, k2 tog, sl 1, k1, psso, yo, [k2 tog, yo] twice, k4; rep from * to last st, k1.
ROW 31 K1, * k4, [yo, sl 1, k1, psso] twice, yo, sl 1, k1, psso, yo, [k2 tog, yo] twice, k3, k2 tog; rep from * to last st, k1.
ROW 32 Purl.

Repeat rows 1 to 32.

CATHEDRAL WINDOW LACE (mauve)

Cast on a multiple of 12 sts plus 1.
ROWS 1, 3 AND 5 P1, * yb, sl 1, k1, psso, k3, yo, p1, yo, k3, k2 tog, p1; rep from * to end.
ROWS 2, 4 AND 6 K1, * p5, k1; rep from * to end.
ROW 7 P1, * yo, k3, k2 tog, p1, yb, sl 1, k1, psso, k3, yo, p1; rep from * to end.

ROW 8 Rep row 2.

ROW 9 P2, yo, k2, k2 tog, p1, yb, sl 1, k1, psso, k2, * yo, p3, yo, k2, k2 tog, p1, yb, sl 1, k1, psso, k2; rep from * to last 2 sts, yo, p2.

ROW 10 K2, p4, k1, p4, * k3, p4, k1, p4; rep from * to last 2 sts, k2.

ROW 11 P3, yo, k1, k2 tog, p1, yb, sl 1, k1, psso, k1, * yo, p5, yo, k1, k2 tog, p1, yb, sl 1, k1, psso, k1; rep from * to last 3 sts, yo, p3.

ROW 12 K3, p3, k1, p3, * k5, p3, k1, p3; rep from * to last 3 sts, k3.

ROW 13 P4, yo, k2 tog, p1, yb, sl 1, k1, psso, * yo, p7, yo, k2 tog, p1, yb, sl 1, k1, psso; rep from * to last 4 sts, yo, p4.

ROW 14 K4, p2, k1, p2, * k7, p2, k1, p2; rep from * to last 4 sts, k4.

ROWS 15, 17 AND 19 Rep row 7.

ROWS 16, 18 AND 20 Rep row 2.

ROW 21 P1, * yb, sl 1, k1, psso, k3, yo, p1, yo, k3, k2 tog, p1; rep from * to end.

ROW 22 Rep row 2.

ROW 23 P1, * yb, sl 1, k1, psso, k2, yo, p3, yo, k2, k2 tog, p1; rep from * to end.

ROW 24 K1, * p4, k3, p4, k1; rep from * to end.

ROW 25 P1, * yb, sl 1, k1, psso, k1, yo, p5, yo, k1, k2 tog, p1; rep from * to end.

ROW 26 K1, * p3, k5, p3, k1; rep from * to end.

ROW 27 P1, * yb, sl 1, k1, psso, yo, p7, yo, k2 tog, p1; rep from * to end.

ROW 28 K1, * p2, k7, p2, k1; rep from * to end.

Repeat rows 1 to 28.

multiple of 12 sts + 1

EYELET PATTERNS

Abbreviations
Knitting abbreviations appear on page 99.

Eyelet patterns are probably the easiest lace design to knit, relying for their effect on simple rows of holes set out in a regular pattern.
The blue and beige samples are both worked over a multiple of five stitches and they can be used to make baby clothes and shawls.

k1	
p1	
yo	
k2 tog	
sl 1, k1, psso	
yb, sl 1, k1, psso	
sl 1, k2 tog, psso	
p2 tog	

TINY BELLS (beige)
Cast on a multiple of 5 sts.

ROWS 1 AND 3 * K3, p2; rep from * to end.

ROWS 2 AND 4 * K2, p3; rep from * to end.

ROW 5 * Yo, sl 1, k2 tog, psso, yo, p2; rep from * to end.

ROW 6 * K2, p3; rep from * to end.

Repeat rows 1 to 6.

multiple of 5 sts

DAINTY ZIGZAGS (blue)
Cast on a multiple of 5 sts.

ROW 1 * K2, p2 tog, yo, k1; rep from * to end.

ROW 2 AND EVERY ALT ROW Purl.

ROWS 3 AND 7 Knit.

ROW 5 * K3, yo, p2 tog; rep from * to end.

ROW 8 Purl.

Repeat rows 1 to 8.

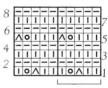

multiple of 5 sts

CHEVRON EYELETS (cream)

multiple of 9 sts

Cast on a multiple of 9 sts.
ROW 1 * K4, yo, sl 1, k1, psso, k3; rep from * to end.
ROW 2 AND EVERY ALT ROW Purl.
ROW 3 * K2, k2 tog, yo, k1, yo, sl 1, k1, psso, k2; rep from * to end.
ROW 5 * K1, k2 tog, yo, k3, yo, sl 1, k1, psso, k1; rep from * to end.
ROW 7 * K2 tog, yo, k5, yo, sl 1, k1, psso; rep from * to end.
ROW 8 Purl.
Repeat rows 1 to 8.

CHEVRON STRIPES (green)

multiple of 12 sts

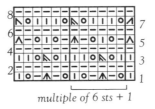

multiple of 6 sts + 1

Like the eyelet patterns, all-over patterns are fairly easy to knit, especially the shell stripes design shown in pink. Try out these patterns using a variety of yarn weights, from fine cotton to heavy, double knitting weight wool, and see what effects are produced.

Cast on a multiple of 12 sts.
ROW 1 * K3, yo, sl 1, k1, psso, k2, k2 tog, yo, k1, yo, sl 1, k1, psso; rep from * to end.
ROWS 2 AND 4 Purl.
ROW 3 * K1, k2 tog, yo, k1, yo, sl 1, k1, psso, k1, k2 tog, yo, k1, yo, sl 1, k1, psso; rep from * to end.
ROW 5 * K2 tog, yo, k3, yo, sl 1, k1, psso, k2 tog, yo, k1, yo, sl 1, k1, psso; rep from * to end.
ROW 6 Purl.
Repeat rows 1 to 6.

ALL-OVER PATTERNS

Abbreviations
Knitting abbreviations appear on page 99.

KNOTTED TRELLIS (cream)
Cast on a multiple of 6 sts plus 1.
ROW 1 K1, * yo, p1, p3 tog, p1, yo, k1;

rep from * to end.
ROW 2 AND EVERY ALT ROW Purl.
ROW 3 K2, yo, sl 1, k2 tog, psso, yo, * k3, yo, sl 1, k2 tog, psso, yo; rep from * to last 2 sts, k2.
ROW 5 P2 tog, p1, yo, k1, yo, p1, * p3 tog, p1, yo, k1, yo, p1; rep from * to last 2 sts, p2 tog.
ROW 7 K2 tog, yo, k3, yo, * sl 1, k2 tog, psso, yo, k3, yo; rep from * to last 2 sts, sl 1, k1, psso.
ROW 8 Purl.
Repeat rows 1 to 8.

LACE BLOCKS (mauve)

multiple of 6 sts + 5

Cast on a multiple of 6 sts plus 5.
ROWS 1, 3, 5 AND 7 K1, * yo, sl 1, k2 tog,
psso, yo, k3; rep from * to last 4 sts,
yo, sl 1, k2 tog, psso, yo, k1.
ROW 2 AND EVERY ALT ROW Purl.
ROWS 9, 11, 13 AND 15 K4, * yo, sl 1, k2 tog,
psso, yo, k3; rep from * to last st, K1.
ROW 16 Purl.
Repeat rows 1 to 16.

LATTICE LACE (green)

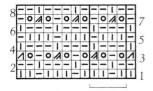

multiple of 4 sts + 1

Cast on a multiple of 4 sts plus 1.
ROW 1 K2, * p1, k3; rep from * to last 3
sts, p1, k2.
ROW 2 P2, * k1, p3; rep from * to last 3
sts, k1, p2.
ROW 3 K2 tog, yo, * p1, yo, k3 tog, yo;
rep from * to last 3 sts, p1, yo, k2 tog.
ROWS 4 AND 6 K1, * p3, k1; rep from * to
end.
ROW 5 P1, * k3, p1; rep from * to end.
ROW 7 P1, * yo, k3 tog, yo, p1; rep from
* to end.
ROW 8 Rep row 2.
Repeat rows 1 to 8.

SHELL STRIPES (pink)

multiple of 7 sts + 1

Cast on a multiple of 7 sts plus 2.
ROW 1 Knit.
ROW 2 Purl.
ROW 3 K2, * yo, p1, p3 tog, p1, yo, k2;
rep from * to end.
ROW 4 Purl.
Repeat rows 1 to 4.

CHEVRON AND WAVE PATTERNS

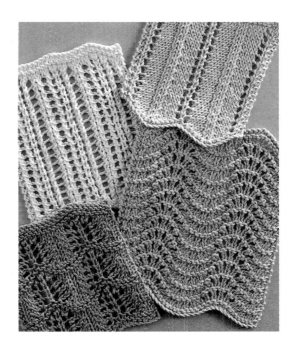

Abbreviations
Knitting abbreviations appear on page 99.

OLD SHALE (pink)

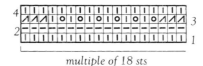

multiple of 18 sts

Cast on a multiple of 18 sts.
ROW 1 Knit.
ROW 2 Purl.
ROW 3 * [K2 tog] 3 times, [yo, k1] 6
times, [k2 tog] 3 times, rep from * to
end.
ROW 4 Knit.
Repeat rows 1 to 4.

VANDYKE LACE (cream)

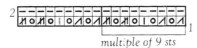

multiple of 9 sts

Cast on a multiple of 9 sts and knit 3
rows before beginning to work pattern.

One of the most traditional groups of knitting patterns, the chevron and wave patterns take on a whole new look when worked in stripes of coloured yarn. Experiment by working the old shale pattern in two-, four-, six- and eight-row stripes using various colour combinations, then use the same colour sequences to work the lacy chevron pattern. The first set of samples will have undulating, wavy lines of colour running across the width, while the second set will show crisp zigzag stripes.

I	k1
−	p1
⊠	sl 1, k2 tog, psso
∧	p2 tog
⋀	p3 tog
⟋	k2 tog
⟍	sl 1, k1, psso
O	yo
⋈	k2 tog tbl
⟋	k3 tog

ROW 1 * [K2 tog, yo] twice, k1, [yo, k2 tog tbl] twice, rep from * to end.
ROW 2 Purl.
Repeat rows 1 and 2.

LACY CHEVRON (peach)

multiple of 13 sts +1

Cast on a multiple of 13 sts plus 1.
ROW 1 * K1, yo, k4, k2 tog, sl 1, k1, psso, k4, yo, rep from * to last st, k1.
ROW 2 Purl.
Repeat rows 1 and 2.

WAVE CREST (fawn)

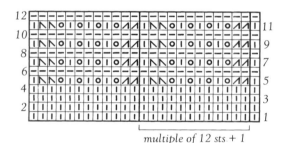

multiple of 12 sts + 1

Cast on a multiple of 12 sts plus 1.
ROW 1 Knit.
ROWS 2, 3 AND 4 Knit.
ROW 5 K1, * [k2 tog] twice, [yo, k1] 3 times, yo, [sl 1, k1, psso] twice, k1, rep from * to end.
ROW 6 Purl.
ROWS 7 TO 12 Rep rows 5 and 6 3 times more.
Repeat rows 1 to 12.

DIAMOND PATTERNS

Abbreviations
Knitting abbreviations appear on page 99.
Special abbreviations for lace diamonds:
p2sso = pass two slipped stitches over.

LACE DIAMONDS (pink)

Cast on a multiple of 6 sts plus 1.
ROW 1 * K1, k2 tog, yo, k1, yo, k2 tog tbl; rep from * to last st, k1.
ROW 2 AND EVERY ALT ROW Purl.
ROW 3 K2 tog, * yo, k3, yo, [sl 1] twice, k1, p2sso; rep from * to last 5 sts, yo, k3, yo, k2 tog tbl.
ROW 5 * K1, yo, k2 tog tbl, k1, k2 tog, yo; rep from * to last st, k1.
ROW 7 K2, * yo, [sl 1] twice, k1, p2sso, yo, k3; rep from * to last 5 sts, yo, [sl 1] twice, k1, p2sso, yo, k2.
ROW 8 Purl.
Repeat rows 1 to 8.

Diamond patterns are very popular and the samples here demonstrate three different treatments of the same theme. The leafy diamonds (shown in green) is an arrangement of diamond-shaped leaves and could be substituted in the Evening Wrap (page 108). In the blue example, the diamond pattern is enhanced by rows of garter stitch, while the lace diamonds pattern (pink) is quick and easy to knit.

LEAFY DIAMONDS (green)

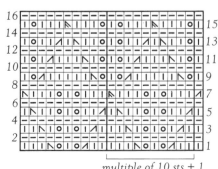

multiple of 10 sts + 1

multiple of 6 sts + 1

Cast on a multiple of 10 sts plus 1.

ROW 1 K3, * k2 tog, yo, k1, yo, sl 1, k1, psso, k5; rep from * to last 8 sts, k2 tog, yo, k1, yo, sl 1, k1, psso, k3.

ROW 2 AND EVERY ALT ROW Purl.

ROW 3 K2, * k2 tog, [k1, yo] twice, k1, sl 1, k1, psso, k3; rep from * to last 9 sts, k2 tog, [k1, yo] twice, k1, sl 1, k1, psso, k2.

ROW 5 K1, * k2 tog, k2, yo, k1, yo, k2, sl 1, k1, psso, k1; rep from * to end.

ROW 7 K2 tog, * k3, yo, k1, yo, k3, sl 1, k2 tog, psso; rep from * to last 9 sts, k3, yo, k1, yo, k3, sl 1, k1, psso.

ROW 9 K1, * yo, sl 1, k1, psso, k5, k2 tog, yo, k1; rep from * to end.

ROW 11 K1, * yo, k1, sl 1, k1, psso, k3, k2 tog, k1, yo, k1; rep from * to end.

ROW 13 K1, * yo, k2, sl 1, k1, psso, k1, k2 tog, k2, yo, k1; rep from * to end.

ROW 15 K1, * yo, k3, sl 1, k2 tog, psso, k3, yo, k1; rep from * to end.

ROW 16 Purl.

Repeat rows 1 to 16.

RIDGED DIAMONDS (blue)

multiple of 10 sts + 3

Cast on a multiple of 10 sts plus 3.

ROW 1 K2, yo, sl 1, k1, psso, k5, k2 tog, yo, * k1, yo, sl 1, k1, psso, k5, k2 tog, yo; rep from * to last 2 sts, k2.

ROW 2 P4, k5, * p5, k5; rep from * to last 4 sts, p4.

ROW 3 K3, * yo, sl 1, k1, psso, k3, k2 tog, yo, k3; rep from * to end.

ROW 4 P5, k3, * p7, k3; rep from * to last 5 sts, p5.

ROW 5 K4, yo, sl 1, k1, psso, k1, k2 tog,

yo, * k5, yo, sl 1, k1, psso, k1, k2 tog, yo; rep from * to last 4 sts, k4.

ROW 6 P6, k1, * p9, k1; rep from * to last 6 sts, p6.

ROW 7 K5, yo, sl 1, k2 tog, psso, yo, * k7, yo, sl 1, k2 tog, psso, yo; rep from * to last 5 sts, k5.

ROW 8 Purl.

ROW 9 K4, k2 tog, yo, k1, yo, sl 1, k1, psso, * k5, k2 tog, yo, k1, yo, sl 1, k1, psso; rep from * to last 4 sts, k4.

ROW 10 K4, p5, * k5, p5; rep from * to last 4 sts, k4.

ROW 11 K3, * k2 tog, yo, k3, yo, sl 1, k1, psso, k3; rep from * to end.

ROW 12 K3, * p7, k3; rep from * to end.

ROW 13 K2, k2 tog, yo, k5, yo, sl 1, k1, psso, * k1, k2 tog, yo, k5, yo, sl 1, k1, psso; rep from * to last 2 sts, k2.

ROW 14 P1, k1, * p9, k1; rep from * to last st, p1.

ROW 15 K1, k2 tog, yo, k7, * yo, sl 1, k2 tog, psso, yo, k7; rep from * to last 3 sts, yo, sl 1, k1, psso, k1.

ROW 16 Purl.

Repeat rows 1 to 16.

	k1
—	p1
C	yo
∕	k2 tog
╲	sl 1, k1, psso
∧	sl 1, k2 tog, psso
∕|	k2 tog tbl
+	[sl 1] twice, k1, p2sso

Lacy knitting contrasts with textured areas formed by working rows of either reverse stocking stitch or garter stitch. Best worked in a fairly substantial yarn to accentuate the textures, the patterns shown produce an interesting surface. Use the patterns to make garments and small household articles such as cushion covers.

LACE AND TEXTURES

Abbreviations

Knitting abbreviations appear on page 99.

	k1
	p1
	yo
	k2 tog
	p2 tog
	sl 1, k1, psso
	sl1, k2 tog, psso
	inc
	cast off 1 stitch
	yo twice

INTERLACED CHEVRONS (peach)

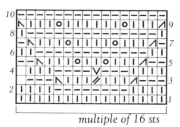

multiple of 16 sts

Cast on a multiple of 16 sts.

ROW 1 Knit.

ROW 2 * K4, p8, k4; rep from * to end.

ROW 3 * P3, k2 tog, k3, yo twice, k3, sl 1, k1, psso, p3; rep from * to end.

ROW 4 * K3, p4, purl into front and back of double yo made on previous row, p4, k3; rep from * to end.

ROW 5 * P2, k2 tog, k3, yo, k2, yo, k3, sl 1, k1, psso, p2; rep from * to end.

ROW 6 * K2, p12, k2; rep from * to end.

ROW 7 * P1, k2 tog, k3, yo, k4, yo, k3, sl 1, k1, psso, p1; rep from * to end.

ROW 8 * K1, p14, k1; rep from * to end.

ROW 9 * K2 tog, k3, yo, k6, yo, k3, sl 1, k1, psso; rep from * to end.

ROW 10 Purl.

Repeat rows 1 to 10.

EGYPTIAN EYELETS (blue)

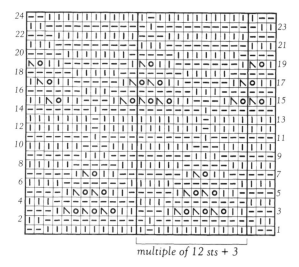

multiple of 12 sts + 3

Cast on a multiple of 12 sts plus 3.

ROW 1 P2, k11, * p1, k11; rep from * to last 2 sts, p2.

ROW 2 K2, p11, * k1, p11; rep from * to last 2 sts, k2.

ROW 3 * P3, k2, [yo, sl 1, k1, psso] 3 times, k1; rep from * to last 3 sts, p3.

ROW 4 K3, * p9, k3; rep from * to end.

ROW 5 P4, k2, [yo, sl 1, k1, psso] twice, k1, * p5, k2, [yo, sl 1, k1, psso] twice, k1; rep from * to last 4 sts, p4.

ROW 6 K4, p7, * k5, p7; rep from * to last 4 sts, k4.

ROW 7 P5, k2, yo, sl 1, k1, psso, k1, * p7, k2, yo, sl 1, k1, psso, k1; rep from * to last 5 sts, p5.

ROW 8 K5, p5, * k7, p5; rep from * to last 5 sts, k5.

ROW 9 P6, k3, * p9, k3; rep from * to last 6 sts, p6.

ROW 10 K6, p3, * k9, p3; rep from * to last 6 sts, k6.

ROW 11 P7, k1, * p11, k1; rep from * to last 7 sts, p7.

ROW 12 K7, p1, * k11, p1; rep from * to last 7 sts, k7.

ROW 13 Rep row 12.

ROW 14 Rep row 11.

ROW 15 K1, [yo, sl 1, k1, psso] twice, k1, p3, * k2, [yo, sl 1, k1, psso] 3 times, k1, p3; rep from * to last 6 sts, k2, yo, sl 1, k1, psso, k2.

ROW 16 Rep row 9.

ROW 17 K2, yo, sl 1, k1, psso, k1, p5, * k2, [yo, sl 1, k1, psso] twice, k1, p5; rep from * to last 5 sts, k2, yo, sl 1, k1, psso, k1.

ROW 18 P5, k5, * p7, k5; rep from * to last 5 sts, p5.

ROW 19 K1, yo, sl 1, k1, psso, k1, p7, * k2, yo, sl 1, k1, psso, k1, p7; rep from * to last 4 sts, k2, yo, sl 1, k1, psso.

ROW 20 P4, k7, * p5, k7; rep from * to last 4 sts, p4.

ROW 21 Rep row 4.

ROW 22 P3, * k9, p3; rep from * to end.

ROW 23 Rep row 2.

ROW 24 Rep row 1.

Repeat rows 1 to 24.

GARTER STITCH CHECKS (*beige*)

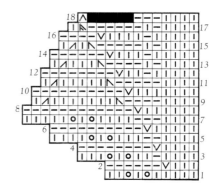

multiple of 16 sts + 2

Cast on a multiple of 16 sts plus 2.

ROWS 1, 3, 5 AND 7 K1, * [sl 1, k1, psso, yo] 4 times, k8; rep from * to last st, k1.

ROWS 2, 4, 6 AND 8 K1, * k8, p8; rep from * to last st, k1.

ROWS 9, 11, 13 AND 15 K1, * k8, [yo, k2 tog] 4 times; rep from * to last st, k1.

ROWS 10, 12, 14 AND 16 K1, * p8, k8; rep from * to last st, k1.

Repeat rows 1 to 16.

RAISED LEAF PATTERNS

Knit four of the triangular raised leaf motifs (cream), arrange them so that the four single leaves touch in the centre, then stitch them together to make a large square. Back the square with matching fabric, or a plain piece of knitting, for use as a cushion cover, or you could work more motifs and stitch the squares together to make a bedspread in the same way as the Victorian bedspread on page 136.

Abbreviations

Knitting abbreviations appear on page 99.

Special abbreviation for leaf motif and shaped leaf edging:

inc = knit once into the front and once into the back of the next stitch.

SHAPED LEAF EDGING (*green*)

Cast on 8 sts.

ROW 1 K5, yo, k1, yo, k2.
ROW 2 P6, inc in next st, k3.
ROW 3 K4, p1, k2, yo, k1, yo, k3.
ROW 4 P8, inc in next st, k4.
ROW 5 K4, p2, k3, yo, k1, yo, k4.
ROW 6 P10, inc in next st, k5.
ROW 7 K4, p3, k4, yo, k1, yo, k5.
ROW 8 P12, inc in next st, k6.
ROW 9 K4, p4, sl 1, k1, psso, k7, k2 tog, k1.
ROW 10 P10, inc in next st, k7.
ROW 11 K4, p5, sl 1, k1, psso, k5, k2 tog, k1.
ROW 12 P8, inc in next st, k2, p1, k5.
ROW 13 K4, p1, k1, p4, sl 1, k1, psso, k3, k2 tog, k1.
ROW 14 P6, inc in next st, k3, p1, k5.
ROW 15 K4, p1, k1, p5, sl 1, k1, psso, k1, k2 tog, k1.
ROW 16 P4, inc in next st, k4, p1, k5.
ROW 17 K4, p1, k1, p6, sl 1, k2 tog, psso, k1.
ROW 18 P2 tog, cast off next 5 sts using p2 tog st when casting off first st, p3, k4.

Repeat rows 1 to 18.

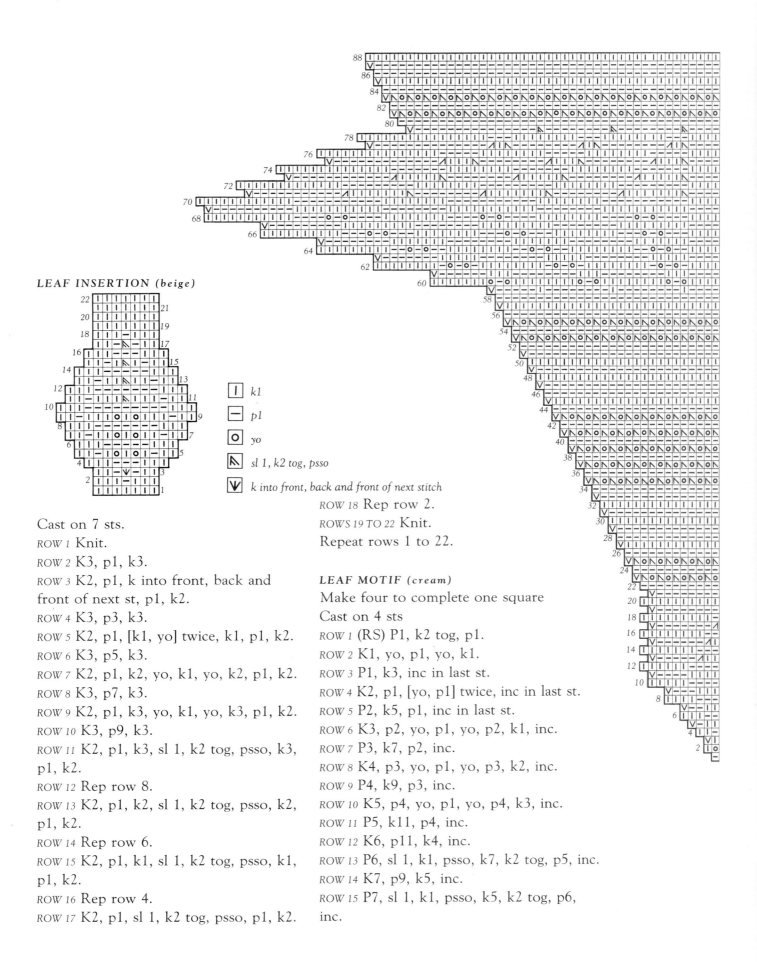

LEAF INSERTION (beige)

$\boxed{\text{I}}$	*k1*
$\boxed{-}$	*p1*
$\boxed{\text{o}}$	*yo*
$\boxed{\text{N}}$	*sl 1, k2 tog, psso*
$\boxed{\text{V}}$	*k into front, back and front of next stitch*

Cast on 7 sts.

ROW 1 Knit.

ROW 2 K3, p1, k3.

ROW 3 K2, p1, k into front, back and front of next st, p1, k2.

ROW 4 K3, p3, k3.

ROW 5 K2, p1, [k1, yo] twice, k1, p1, k2.

ROW 6 K3, p5, k3.

ROW 7 K2, p1, k2, yo, k1, yo, k2, p1, k2.

ROW 8 K3, p7, k3.

ROW 9 K2, p1, k3, yo, k1, yo, k3, p1, k2.

ROW 10 K3, p9, k3.

ROW 11 K2, p1, k3, sl 1, k2 tog, psso, k3, p1, k2.

ROW 12 Rep row 8.

ROW 13 K2, p1, k2, sl 1, k2 tog, psso, k2, p1, k2.

ROW 14 Rep row 6.

ROW 15 K2, p1, k1, sl 1, k2 tog, psso, k1, p1, k2.

ROW 16 Rep row 4.

ROW 17 K2, p1, sl 1, k2 tog, psso, p1, k2.

ROW 18 Rep row 2.

ROWS 19 TO 22 Knit.

Repeat rows 1 to 22.

LEAF MOTIF (cream)

Make four to complete one square

Cast on 4 sts

ROW 1 (RS) P1, k2 tog, p1.

ROW 2 K1, yo, p1, yo, k1.

ROW 3 P1, k3, inc in last st.

ROW 4 K2, p1, [yo, p1] twice, inc in last st.

ROW 5 P2, k5, p1, inc in last st.

ROW 6 K3, p2, yo, p1, yo, p2, k1, inc.

ROW 7 P3, k7, p2, inc.

ROW 8 K4, p3, yo, p1, yo, p3, k2, inc.

ROW 9 P4, k9, p3, inc.

ROW 10 K5, p4, yo, p1, yo, p4, k3, inc.

ROW 11 P5, k11, p4, inc.

ROW 12 K6, p11, k4, inc.

ROW 13 P6, sl 1, k1, psso, k7, k2 tog, p5, inc.

ROW 14 K7, p9, k5, inc.

ROW 15 P7, sl 1, k1, psso, k5, k2 tog, p6, inc.

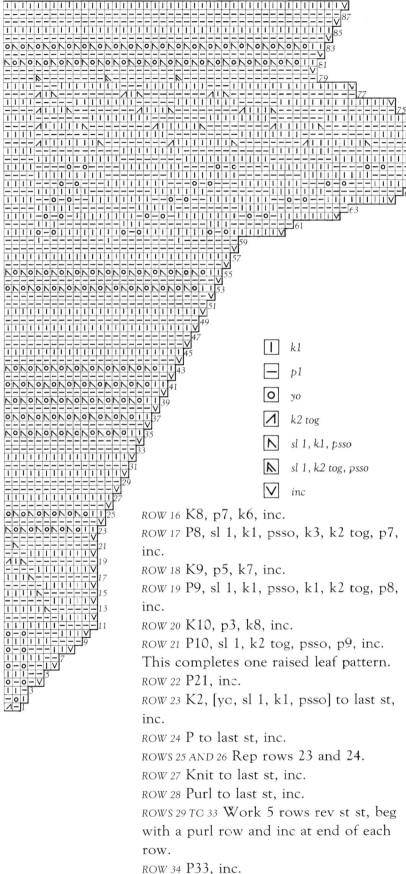

Key

		k1
−	p1
o	yo
⟋	k2 tog
⟍	sl 1, k1, psso
⋀	sl 1, k2 tog, psso
V	inc

ROW 16 K8, p7, k6, inc.

ROW 17 P8, sl 1, k1, psso, k3, k2 tog, p7, inc.

ROW 18 K9, p5, k7, inc.

ROW 19 P9, sl 1, k1, psso, k1, k2 tog, p8, inc.

ROW 20 K10, p3, k8, inc.

ROW 21 P10, sl 1, k2 tog, psso, p9, inc. This completes one raised leaf pattern.

ROW 22 P21, inc.

ROW 23 K2, [yo, sl 1, k1, psso] to last st, inc.

ROW 24 P to last st, inc.

ROWS 25 AND 26 Rep rows 23 and 24.

ROW 27 Knit to last st, inc.

ROW 28 Purl to last st, inc.

ROWS 29 TO 33 Work 5 rows rev st st, beg with a purl row and inc at end of each row.

ROW 34 P33, inc.

ROWS 35 TO 44 Rep rows 23 and 24 5 times.

ROW 45 Knit to last st, inc.

ROW 46 Purl to last st, inc.

ROWS 47 TO 51 Work 5 rows rev st st, beg with a purl row and inc at end of each row.

ROW 52 P51, inc.

ROWS 53 TO 56 Rep rows 23 and 24 twice.

ROW 57 Knit to last st, inc.

ROW 58 Purl to last st, inc.

(59 sts)

ROW 59 P7, [k1, p8] 5 times, k1, p5, inc.

ROW 60 K7, [yo, p1, yo, k8] to end, ending last rep k6, inc.

ROW 61 P8, [k3, p8] 5 times, k3, p6, inc.

ROW 62 K8, [p1, yo, p1, yo, p1, k8] to end, ending last rep k7, inc.

ROW 63 P9, [k5, p8] 5 times, k5, p7, inc. Continue in this way working 6 raised leaf patterns as before and inc at the end of every row until there are 80 sts on the needle.

NEXT ROW P79, inc.

NEXT 4 ROWS Rep rows 23 and 24 twice.

NEXT ROW Knit to last st, inc.

NEXT 2 ROWS Purl to last st, inc.

NEXT ROW Knit to last st, inc.

(89 sts)

Cast off loosely knitwise.

This completes one triangle. To make one square motif, work three more triangles in the same way and stitch together, placing the cast-on edges at the centre of the square.

USEFUL
SUPPLIERS

UNITED KINGDOM

MAIL ORDER
Framecraft
372–376 Summer Lane
Hockley
Birmingham
B19 3QA

Hollyoak Mail Order Supplies
Cogshall Lane
Comberbach
Cheshire
CW9 6BS
(equipment, pattern books and yarns)

The Readicut Wool Co
Terry Mills
Ossett
West Yorkshire
WF5 9SA
(equipment, accessories and yarns)

William Hall (Monsall) Ltd
177 Stanley Road
Cheadle Hulme
Cheshire
SK8 6RF
(natural and dyed yarns, including linen and cotton)

Texere Yarns
College Mill
Barkerend Road
Bradford
West Yorkshire
BD3 9AQ
(natural silk and cotton yarns, dyed silk, cotton and wool yarns)

Jamieson and Smith
90 North Road
Lerwick
ZE1 0PQ
Shetland Isles
(Shetland wool yarn)

MANUFACTURERS
Jaeger Handknitting
McMullen Road
Darlington
Durham
DL1 1YH
(cotton and wool yarns)

Rowan Yarns
Green Lane Mill
Washpit
Holmfirth
West Yorkshire
HD7 1RW
(cotton and wool yarns)

HG Twilley Ltd
Roman Mills
Stamford
Lincolnshire
PE9 1BG
(cotton yarn)

Coats Leisure Crafts Group
39 Durham Street
Kinning Park
Glasgow
G41 1BS
(cotton and wool yarns)

DMC Creative World
Pullman Road
Wigston
Leicester
LE8 2DY
(cotton)